photographs by
Georgia Glynn Smith

Quadrille
PUBLISHING

PEGGY PORSCHEN

Cake Chic

Stylish cookies and cakes for all occasions

To my wonderful husband Bryn
and to my family, with all my love

First published in 2009 by
Quadrille Publishing Limited,
Alhambra House, 27-31 Charing Cross Road,
London WC2H OLS

Reprinted in 2009
10 9 8 7 6 5 4 3 2

Editorial Director: Jane O'Shea
Creative Director: Helen Lewis
Editor and Project Manager: Lewis Esson
Designers: Katherine Case, Nicola Davidson
Photography: Georgia Glynn Smith
Stylist: Vicky Sullivan
Production: Vincent Smith, Aysun Hughes

Cataloguing in Publication Data: a catalogue record for this
book is available from the British Library

ISBN 978 184400 710 3

Printed and bound in China.

Contents

Cookies

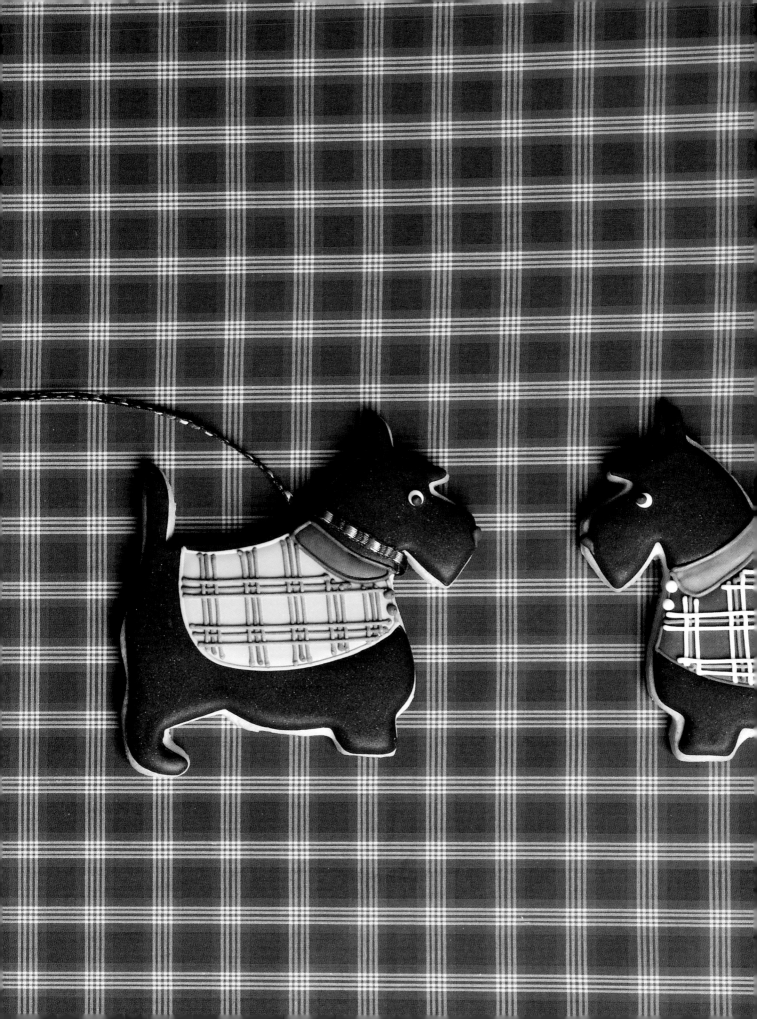

MAKES 12
PAIRS

Ballerina pumps

When Chanel commissioned me to design party favours to celebrate the 50th anniversary of the ballerina pump I was delighted – cookies couldn't get more couture! They were served at a celebrity-studded tea party with each cookie bearing a guest's name iced along the middle.

INGREDIENTS

12 pairs of ballet pump cookies made from ½ recipe quantity Vanilla cookie dough (page 110)
about 400g royal icing (page 132)
ivory, pink, dark brown and black food colours
small amount of water

EQUIPMENT

ballet pump templates (page 144)
paper piping bags (page 134)
small bowls
small palette knife
cling-film or resealable plastic bag, to cover the icing
pair of scissors
6 sheets of wrapping paper
6 gift boxes (optional)
About 6m ribbon, 15mm width (optional)

1 Start by mixing your icing colours, you will need:
2 piping bags filled with nude royal icing (mix ivory, pink and dark brown) – one soft-peak and one runny (page 132).
2 piping bags filled with black icing – one soft-peak and one runny
1 piping bag filled with runny cream-coloured icing (use ivory)
2 piping bags filled with ivory icing – one soft-peak and one runny.

2 Begin by piping the nude-coloured outlines of the pumps using soft-peak icing. Snip a small tip off the bag and pipe the inner and outer shapes of the pump in a steady and smooth line (see 1). Repeat for all the pumps and let dry.

3 Using the runny nude-coloured icing, flood the space between the two outlines on each cookie (see 2) and let the icing dry.

4 Outline the shoe tips using soft-peak black icing (see 3).

5 Flood the central part of the cookies with the runny cream-coloured icing and let dry (see 3).

6 Flood the centres of the tips with runny black icing (see 4). Let dry.

7 Once all the colours on the cookies are dry, pipe the black bow detail using soft-peak icing (see 5).

8 For a name tag, pipe a rectangle across the cream-coloured centre using soft-peak ivory icing and flood it with runny ivory icing. Let dry.

9 You can pipe a guest's name across the tag using black soft-peak icing. If you like, wrap each pair in pretty paper, put in gift boxes and tie with ribbon.

 **1**  **2**  **3**  **4**  **5**

little Black Dress

Every girl has one – what does yours look like? Mine was inspired by a 1950s' vintage Dior design. The secret of this cookie is to keep the actual dress design quite simple and then to add a pretty finishing touch by tying a chic little satin bow around the waist to match your party's colour scheme. They make the perfect treat for any fashionista tea party!

INGREDIENTS
12 dress cookies (about 8 x 12.5cm) made from 1 recipe quantity of sugar cookie dough (page 110)
about 400g royal icing (page 132)
black food colour
small amount of water

EQUIPMENT
dress cookie cutter (about 8 x 12.5cm)
small bowl
small palette knife
paper piping bags (page 134)
cling-film or resealable plastic bag, to cover the icing
60cm brightly coloured satin ribbon, 3mm width

1 Put the royal icing in a small bowl and mix it with black food colour to a deep black. Add a small amount of water until the icing is soft-peak consistency (page 132). Put some into a piping bag. Keep the remaining icing covered.

2 Snip a small tip off the bag and pipe the outlines of the dresses in a steady smooth line (see piping techniques on page 135). Keep the piping bag covered in a plastic bag or cling-film until later to prevent it from drying out.

3 Dilute the remaining icing with a few drops of water to a runny consistency (page 132). Put it in a fresh piping bag.

4 Again, snip the tip off the bag and flood the cookie centres with the runny icing, being careful not to overflow the sides. Let dry.

5 Once dry, pipe the details on your dresses using the remaining soft-peak royal icing.

6 Once completely dry, tie the ribbons around the waists with a little bow at the front.

best in *Show*

These Scotties make great gifts for dog lovers! You can bake them in the shape of your favourite breed, from Afghans to Salukis. There are plenty of different dog cookie cutters (see the suppliers list on page 137).

INGREDIENTS
12 dog cookies made from 1 quantity
   of vanilla cookie dough (page 110)
about 600g royal icing (page 132)
black, brown, ivory, purple,
   dark-pink and green food colours
small amount of water

EQUIPMENT
dog cookie cutter (about 11 x 8.5cm)
small bowls
small palette knife
paper piping bags (page 134)
cling-film or resealable plastic bag,
   to cover the icing

1 Colour about 300g royal icing black. Add a little water until a soft-peak consistency is reached (page 132). Put a little in a piping bag and cover the rest.

2 Snip a small tip off the bag and pipe the outlines, leaving space for jacket and collar. Pipe all black outlines first (see 1). If icing is left in the bag, keep in the resealable bag.

3 Make the remaining black icing runny (page 132) by adding a little water. Put in a fresh bag.

4 Snip a tip off the bag and fill the centres of the dogs with the runny icing (see 2), being careful not to overflow the sides. Let dry.

5 Prepare your icing for the jackets:
1 bag with a little brown soft-peak;
1 bag with a little brown runny;
1 bag with a little ivory soft-peak;
1 bag with a little purple soft-peak;
about 2 bags with purple runny;
1 bag with a little dark-pink soft-peak;

about 2 bags with dark-pink runny;
1 bag with a little green soft-peak;
about 2 bags with green runny.

6 Pipe the outlines for the jacket collars and jackets using soft-peak icing as shown (see 2). Let dry.

7 Flood the centres of the jackets with the corresponding runny colour (see 3) and let dry.

8 Flood the collars with the runny colour (see 4). Let dry.

9 Using soft-peak icing, pipe the outlines for the jacket and the collar (see 5), followed by the tartan designs. Mix and match colours as shown or to your taste (see 6). Let one colour dry first before you pipe a different one on top.

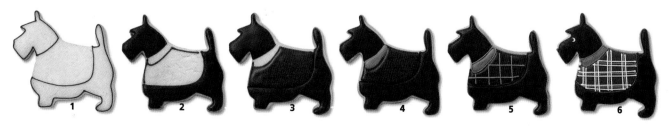

pretty Bows

These suit girly get-togethers or bridal and baby showers. You can keep them plain with just a touch of lustre, decorate them with dots or embellish them with sugar pearls for a more sophisticated affair. They also look very chic in black and white – great for a cocktail party.

INGREDIENTS

12 small bow-shaped cookies (about 6cm) made from ½ recipe quantity of vanilla cookie dough (page 110)
300g royal icing (page 132)
ivory, pink, blue and yellow food colours
small amount of water
ivory sugar pearls (Almond Art)
pearl lustre spray (PME)

EQUIPMENT

bow cookie cutter (about 6cm)
small bowl
small palette knife
small kitchen knife
paper piping bags (page 134)
cling-film or resealable plastic bag, to cover the icing

FOR THE THIN PEARL-STUDDED BOWS

1 To make about 4 of these, preheat the oven to 180°C/gas 4.

2 Roll a small amount of dough to about 4mm thick. Cut out 4 strips 6mm wide and 14cm long.

3 Fold to make a bow as below and pinch in the middle.

4 Bake for about 6-8 minutes with the 8 cut-out bow cookies. Allow to cool on a wire rack.

5 Fill a piping bag with a little soft-peak (page 132) white royal icing and pipe a thin line all along each of the pearl-studded bow cookies.

6 While the icing is still wet, stick a row of white sugar pearls on top of the icing. Let dry.

FOR THE CUT-OUT BOWS

7 Prepare your icing colours and piping bags. You will need:

2 bags with pale-pink icing – 1 with soft-peak and 1 runny (page 132);
2 bags with pale-blue icing – 1 with soft-peak and 1 with runny;
2 bags with pale-yellow icing – 1 with soft-peak and 1 with runny;
1 bag with soft-peak ivory icing.

8 Start by piping the outlines: snip a small tip off the bag and pipe around the bow outlines in a steady smooth line. Let dry. If you have any icing left in your bags, keep them in resealable bags.

9 Flood the bow centres with runny icing in corresponding colours and let dry.

10 Pipe the outlines using the soft-peak icing in corresponding colours and place a cluster of sugar pearls in the centre. Alternatively, use soft-peak ivory icing to pipe very small dots instead of the outlines.

11 Finish by spraying a light dusting of pearl spray over the dry cookies.

Christmas baubles

These beautiful baubles make ornaments for your Christmas tree that are both festive and sophisticated. They look amazing in any colour combination, so for something more traditional use red, green and white; or, for a bold statement, try fuchsia, burnt-orange and deep purple. Gingerbread has a very long shelf-life, so these decorative cookies can also make wonderful gifts and stocking-fillers.

INGREDIENTS
6 small (about 6cm) and 6 large
    (about 11cm) tree ornament
    cookies with holes at the top
    made from ½ recipe quantity of
    gingerbread dough (page 112)
about 600g royal icing (page 132)
pink, purple and ivory food colours
small amount of water
silver sugar balls

EQUIPMENT
small bowls
small palette knife
paper piping bags (page 134)
cling-film or resealable plastic bags
    to cover the icing
about 6m purple satin ribbon, 5mm
    width

1 Prepare your icing colours: for 2 small and 2 large baubles of each colour (pink, purple and ivory) you will need 1 small piping bag filled with soft-peak icing and 1 slightly larger piping bag filled with runny icing (page 132.)

2 First pipe all the outlines of the baubles using the soft-peak icing.

3 Then flood the bauble centres using the runny icing in the corresponding colours. Let dry.

4 Once dry, pipe the details on top and embellish the designs with silver sugar pearls where required while that icing is still wet. Let the icing dry completely.

5 Once dry, cut the ribbon into 12 lengths, thread them through the holes in the baubles and tie them into a bow. Handle the cookies with care as they can be very fragile.

Silhouette cookies

These timelessly stylish silhouette cookies make great party favours for birthdays, engagements and, in particular, weddings. Using profile photographs of the bride and groom – or guests – is a great way to personalise these wonderful gifts. Imagine the fun and laughter as your guests try to find their own silhouette! I chose chocolate on pastels for a retro-feel, but they also look very chic in black and white.

INGREDIENTS

12 oval (about 10cm) cookies made from ½ recipe quantity gingerbread dough (see page 112)
about 500g royal icing (see page 132)
dark-brown, blue, pink and ivory food colours
small amount of water
small amount of white vegetable fat
gold lustre

EQUIPMENT

small bowls
small palette knife
paper piping bags (see page 134)
sheet of cellophane or plastic sleeve
greaseproof paper
pencil
5cm diameter face silhouette prints
soft artist's brush for dusting
cling-film or resealable plastic bags, to cover the icing

1 For the silhouettes you need 1 small piping bag of brown soft-peak icing and 1 slightly larger bag filled with brown runny icing (page 132).

2 To make your own silhouette templates, place a piece of greaseproof paper over the photographs and trace the outlines with a pencil. Then place a sheet of cellophane on top and rub in very thinly with the vegetable fat. Place them on a flat surface or a tray.

3 Using the soft-peak brown icing, first trace all the outlines of the silhouette templates, then flood the centres with the runny brown icing. Let them dry overnight.

4 Next day, to ice the cookies, divide the remaining icing equally into 3 bowls and mix one each with pink, blue, and ivory (use a lot of the ivory to make it very creamy) food colours respectively. Add a little water, if required, to get a soft-peak consistency. Fill a small amount of each colour into a piping bag and keep the remaining icing covered to prevent it drying out.

5 Use these bags to outline 4 cookies in each colour and squeeze the leftover icing back into their bowls. Add more water to make the icing runny, fill each colour into a new bag and flood the cookie centres.

6 Where required, let small dots of an opposite colour drop into the icing while it is still wet, to create a spotty background pattern. Let the cookies dry completely.

7 For the golden cookies, brush the creamy golden iced cookies generously with the gold lustre, using a soft artist's brush.

8 Once the silhouettes are dry, stick them on top of the cookies with dabs of royal icing.

**MAKES 30
COOKIES**

i want

These retro cookies, inspired by traditional sweets, add a fun factor to any party. For younger guests, mix primary colours; for grown-up parties, keep them classy by using, say, black, white and bright pink. They make great give-away treats for guests. Pile them into an old-fashioned sweet jar, mixed with sweets, or wrap in cellophane and decorate with ribbon.

INGREDIENTS

15 round cookies (about 3cm in diameter) and 15 round (or oval) cookies (about 5cm in diameter), made from 1 quantity of Sugar cookie dough (see page 110)

black and pink food colours

about 600g royal icing (see page 132)

small amount of water

about 20g each white, black and pink sugar balls

EQUIPMENT

selection of small bowls

small palette knife

paper piping bags (see page 134)

cling-film or a damp cloth to cover the icing

1 Choose the colours for your cookies and divide the icing equally into bowls, one per colour. Using a clean palette knife each time, mix each one with a small amount of food colour to the desired tone and add a little water until the icing has soft-peak consistency (page 132). Fill a piping bag of each.

2 Snip a small tip off the bag containing your chosen colour for outlines and pipe the outline of each cookie in a steady smooth line. When not in use, cover the bags with cling film or a plastic bag to prevent drying out.

3 Once the icing outlines are dry, flood the centres: dilute a small amount of the required icing colour with some water to runny consistency (page 132) and use to fill a piping bag. Snip a small tip of the bag and pipe the liquid icing into the centres, being careful not to overflow the sides (see 1).

4 If flooding sections in different colours, let one colour dry first before flooding the next, to avoid them flowing together.

5 While the flooded icing is still wet, pipe the white dots on black-iced cookies to be dotted, so they sink into the background (see 2), and sprinkle cookies being decorated with sugar balls with the appropriately coloured balls (see 3).

6 Once the other cookies are dry, pipe outlines and stripes, etc., in the required colours, using soft-peak icing.

Mini Cakes

Damask delights

Damask patterns have made a huge comeback and I love the eclectic mix of different pattern and colour possibilities. My little damask cakes make super-stylish treats for any cocktail party, presented on a colourful tray. These colours work particularly well for guests of both sexes, but they would also look beautiful in softer shades or tone-on-tone combinations.

INGREDIENTS

16 fondant fancies made from a 20cm square Victoria sponge flavoured to your choice (page 129), dipped in aubergine-coloured fondant icing (page 130) made using purple and claret food colours

about 200g royal icing (page 132)

claret, baby-blue and lemon-yellow food colours (I used the ones from Sugar Flair)

small amount of water

EQUIPMENT

16 silver metallic muffin cases

2 small bowls

small palette knife

paper piping bags (page 134)

cling-film

1 Place the fondant fancies in the silver paper cases as described on page 130.

2 Place half the royal icing in a small bowl and, using a palette knife, mix it with the claret food colour, then add a few drops of water until the icing has reached soft-peak consistency (page 132).

3 Fill some of the icing into a piping bag and keep the rest in the bowl, covered with cling film to prevent it from drying out so that you can use it later, if required.

4 Snip a small tip off the piping bag and pipe the pink design on half the fondant fancies.

5 Repeat steps 2 and 3 using baby-blue and lemon-yellow to mix a bright lime-green colour and pipe that on the other half of the fancies.

**MAKES 10
MINI CAKES**

Cameo cakes

If there was a modern Marie-Antoinette, these would most definitely be her favourite cakes. I used antique cameo brooches as inspiration for these ultra-chic cakes. Perfect for tea parties in Versailles, don't you think? You can also make your own moulds from a vintage piece of jewellery, using a specialist food-safe moulding gel.

INGREDIENTS

10 oval miniature cakes, made from a 30cm square sponge (page 114), flavoured to your choice, covered with 1.5kg marzipan and a thin layer of shell-pink sugar paste (about 1kg)

about 500g white sugar paste

small amount of gum tragacanth

small amount of white vegetable fat

black food colour

icing sugar or cornflour, for dusting

edible glue

small amount of royal icing (page 132)

EQUIPMENT

cling-film

2 or 3 rubber cameo moulds (here 9007 and 9003 from Aldaval – and the other one I bought on eBay)

small rolling pin

small kitchen knife

small non-stick plastic board

oval cutter about 4 x 5cm

Stayfresh multi-mat

small artist's brush

paper piping bags (page 134)

about 3m black satin ribbon, 15mm width

1 Knead the white sugar paste with a small amount of gum tragacanth until stretchy, smooth and pliable. Wrap in cling film until required, to prevent it drying out.

2 Lightly grease each of the cameo moulds with a small quantity of white vegetable fat.

3 Roll a hazelnut-sized piece of the white sugar paste for each mould into a ball, then place it over the centre of the prepared mould and push it thoroughly into the mould. Level out the top with a small rolling

pin and trim off the excess paste at the edges with a small kitchen knife.

4 To release the paste from the mould, bend it inside out and the paste should drop out. Repeat for the remaining 9 cameos. Let dry.

5 Mix the remaining white sugar paste with black food colour.

6 On a plastic board lightly dusted with icing sugar or cornflour, roll out the black sugar paste to a thickness of about 2mm.

7 Using the oval cutter, cut out 10 ovals of black sugar paste (one for each cake). Brush with edible glue an area on top of each cake about the same size as the oval and place one of the black sugar paste ovals on top of each cake. Keep those not being worked on under the multi-mat to prevent them drying out.

8 Using edible glue in the same way, now stick the cameos on top of the sugar paste ovals as well.

9 To make the bows, cut a few thin strips of black paste with a knife

and shape into loops, securing the knot with a tiny brushing of edible glue. Let dry for about 30 minutes.

10 Meanwhile, mix the royal icing with a little bit of water to a soft-peak consistency (page 132) and fill a piping bag with it.

11 Cut the black ribbon into lengths that will fit around the base of each cake and stick in place at the back with a dab of royal icing.

12 Snip a small piece off the tip of the piping bag and pipe the different swag and pearl borders around the base – half on, half off the ribbon. This will give you a great visual effect.

13 Next, while the icing is still wet, pipe a pearl border around the black edge of each cameo and then place a bow either at the top or the bottom of the cameo.

14 You can finish some of the bows by piping dropping pearls down from the knot.

mini *Orangery* cakes

These cakes are inspired by the ornate architecture of some beautiful orangeries I have been lucky enough to visit. A bit of time and patience may be needed to master the dome-making technique, but they are well worth the effort. The caged blooms could work well at a coming-of-age or engagement party.

INGREDIENTS

18 round miniature (5cm) cakes, flavoured to your choice, covered with 850g marzipan and a thin layer of white sugar paste (about 1kg), made from a 30cm square sponge (see page 114)

small amount of white vegetable fat

about 250g royal icing (page 132)

about 200g white sugar paste

about 200g white sugar florist paste (SK)

claret (Sugar Flair), moss-green (Wilton) and grape/violet (Sugar Flair) food colours

EQUIPMENT

a few dome-shaped stainless steel pastry moulds, 6cm in diameter

oven tray

several small plastic bowls

small palette knife

paper piping bags (see page 134)

pair of scissors

foam mat

cling film

clear plastic sleeves (from office suppliers)

small non-stick plastic board

small rolling pin

small stephanotis blossom cutter

Dresden tool

about 5m Malibu blue satin ribbon (Berrisfords), 15mm width

Stayfresh multi-mat

small rose leaf cutter

flower foam pad

rose leaf veining mat

TO MAKE THE DOMES (A DAY AHEAD)

1 Rub a little fat over the moulds. Set on the lightly greased oven tray.

2 Put the icing in a bowl with a few drops of water and work to a fairly stiff but smooth piping consistency. Fill it into a piping bag.

3 Snip a small tip off the bag and pipe thin lines from top to bottom all around the dome. Finish at the bottom with small dots. Pipe drapes halfway down every other line. Finish the top with a piped design as shown, and a piped pearl. Repeat for the other domes. Let dry overnight, keeping the leftover icing in the bag inside a resealable bag (see 1).

4 Next day, preheat your oven to 50–100°C/gas ¼) and place the trays in it for about 10 minutes until the steel is very warm, almost hot. This melts the fat to release the cages.

5 As the tray comes from the oven, lift the domes off the moulds very carefully and place on the foam mat.

TO MAKE THE FLOWERS

6 Knead the sugar paste and the florist paste together to create a slightly stronger yet soft and flexible modelling paste. It is not as strong as florist paste, but works well for making rose petals and leaves.

7 Divide the paste into thirds. In a bowl, mix two-thirds with claret food colour to a deep cerise shade. Keep it wrapped in cling film to prevent it from drying out. Divide the remaining third in half and, in separate small bowls, colour one half green, the other half violet. Also keep these wrapped until later.

8 For the rosebuds, lightly grease the inside of the plastic pockets and make 1 large and 1 small rosebud per cake. To make each rosebud, you need 3 hazelnut-sized balls of marzipan and one twice as large. Place between the sheets of plastic and push the large piece down sideways to make it longer, and then flatten one long side with your

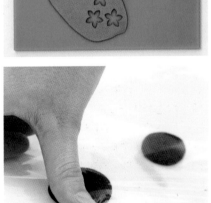

thumb until very thin (see 3). For the other petals, begin to push one of the smaller pieces down with your thumb, starting from the centre to one side, until it forms a round petal, with one thick and one thin sides. Repeat with the other balls. Taking the large petal first, roll it into a spiral shape, thin side up (see 4). Take one of the smaller petals, thin side up, and lay it around the the centre over the seam. Then tuck the second petal slightly inside the first and the third into the second petal and squeeze it around the centre (see 5). Slightly curve the edges of the petals out with your fingertips. Ensure they are small enough to fit under the cages. Keep under the multi-mat as you make them.

9 To make the leaves, roll out the green paste to about 1mm thick and stamp out 2 leaves per cake (36 in total), using the small rose leaf cutter. Place them on a flower foam pad and gently stretch and thin the edges with the Dresden tool. Press each leaf in the rose leaf veiner and shape slightly with your fingers for a natural look. Keep under the multi-mat as you make them.

10 For the little violet-coloured blossoms, roll a small piece of violet paste out on the plastic board until about 1mm thick (see 2). You will need to cut out about 3 blossoms per cake (54 in total)

11 While the blossom is still soft, place it on the foam pad and run

the Dresden tool along each petal to emboss it. Let them dry.

12 Once dry, pipe a small dot of the reserved white (or colour it appropriately) icing into the flower centres.

TO ASSEMBLE AND FINISH
13 Cut the ribbon into pieces to fit the base of each cake and attach with a little royal icing at the back.

14 Arrange a cluster of sugar rosebuds, leaves and blossoms on the top of each cake, leaving an edge on which the domes can rest.

15 Finally, pipe a few dots of icing around the edge and carefully place the dome on top. You can use trimmings to make extra rosebuds, leaves and blossoms for decoration.

**MAKES 8
MINI CAKES**

mini *Monogram* cakes

This is a great and relatively easy idea for making personalised cakes for any occasion. For example, you can use a single monogram, a number to celebrate someone's birthday or the interlinked initials of a couple for a wedding anniversary. You can use different letters to spell out a message or even use the cakes as table place cards for your guests using their initials. With a generous 7.5cm size, these cakes can also be served as desserts. The templates on pages 141-144 will provide you with simple but chic alphabet and border designs so that you can make up your own variations.

INGREDIENTS

8 round marbled miniature cakes, with a diameter of 7.5cm made from a 30cm square marbled sponge cake (page 118) layered with vanilla buttercream, then covered with marzipan and pale-brown sugar paste (page 126)

about 300g royal icing

dark-brown food colour

small amount of water

EQUIPMENT

alphabet and border templates (pages 142-3)

greaseproof paper

pencil

scriber

small bowl

small palette knife

paper piping bags (page 134)

cling-film

about 2.5m dark-brown gros grain ribbon, 25mm width

1

2

3

1 Choose your monogram letter(s) or numeral(s) from the template and trace on to a small piece of greaseproof paper with a pencil (see 1).

2 Centre the paper on top of each cake and carefully trace through the paper on to the icing by pricking with the scriber needle (see 1).

3 Choose a border design from page 142 and also trace this on to the paper as before. Place it neatly around the edge of the cake and trace it on to the cake as well.

4 Prepare a piping bag filled with soft-peak icing and one with runny dark-brown icing (page 132).

5 Snip a fine tip off the bag of soft-peak icing and pipe along the outside of the letters (see 2) and the border (see 3).

6 Then use the runny icing to flood the middles of the monograms.

7 Place the ribbon around the bases and attach with small dabs of icing.

Cherry Blossom bites

Cherry blossoms are among my favourite flowers as they are so delicate, fresh and pretty. These fondant fancies would suit a tea party marking the arrival of spring. Not only do they look divine, but they also taste heavenly – the fruity-fresh Morello cherry jam and the bittersweet chocolate perfectly complement one another and the smooth fondant icing helps create a wonderful melt-in-the-mouth texture.

INGREDIENTS

16 fondant fancies made from a 20cm square Victoria sponge (page 129) flavoured with vanilla, filled with one layer of Morello cherry jam, then dipped in pastel-pink fondant icing (page 130).

about 50g white sugar florist paste (I use Squires Kitchen)

claret food colour (I use the paste colour from Sugar Flair)

small amount of white vegetable fat

small amount of cornflour for dusting

200g couverture chocolate buttons

pink edible dust colour (from Sugar Flair or Squires Kitchen)

1 teaspoon royal icing (page 132)

small amount of water

EQUIPMENT

small bowl (microwaveable)

small palette knife

small non-stick plastic board

small rolling pin

foam flower pad

five-petal flower cutters in 3 sizes, ranging from about 2cm to 4cm in diameter (I use the ones from Orchard)

Stayfresh multi-mat

bone tool

plastic palette

fine artist's brush

paper piping bags (page 134)

pair of scissors

cling film or resealable plastic bag

microwaveable bowl

microwave cooker

digital thermometer

J-cloth

wire rack

greaseproof paper

MAKE ABOUT 30 CHERRY BLOSSOMS (ABOUT 10 IN EACH SIZE) AT LEAST ONE DAY IN ADVANCE

1 Mix the sugar florist paste with a tiny drop of claret food colour to a very pale pink. If the paste is very stiff and sticky, add a dab of the white vegetable fat and knead it until it is smooth and pliable.

2 Lightly grease the non-stick plastic board with a small amount of the white vegetable fat and roll out the pale pink paste until it is about 1mm thick. Cut out the flower shapes using the five-petal flower cutters and remove the trimmings. (Keep these wrapped in cling film or in a resealable plastic bag to prevent the paste from drying out.)

3 Place one flower shape at a time on the foam flower pad and keep the remaining flower shapes on the plastic board covered with the Stayfresh multi-mat to prevent them from drying out.

4 To shape the petals, move the thicker end of the bone tool gently across each one until it is thin and slightly frilly, being very careful not to tear it.

5 Once all the petals have been shaped, place the flower into the well of the plastic palette that has been lightly dusted with cornflour to prevent the flower from sticking to it.

6 Repeat steps 3-5 for all the remaining flowers and let them dry for at least 4 hours or overnight.

7 Once dry, lightly dust the flower centres with the dark-pink dust colour using the fine artist's brush. To make the colour dust slightly paler, you can mix it with a small amount of cornflour.

8 Mix about half the royal icing with the claret food colour and a small amount of water to a soft-peak consistency (page 132). Put it in a paper piping bag, snip a small tip off the bag to pipe small dots in the centre of each flower.

TO TEMPER THE CHOCOLATE

9 Place 150g of the chocolate buttons in a microwaveable bowl and melt it gently on medium heat. Be careful not to overheat it, as chocolate can burn easily. Check the temperature with a thermometer; it should be melted and between 44 and 48°C.

10 Once it has reached the required temperature, stir the remaining chocolate buttons into the melted

chocolate to cool it down to about 28°C while stirring.

11 Once the chocolate has cooled down, gently warm it up again to 32-34°C and the chocolate should now be tempered. You can test it by dipping the blade of a palette knife into the chocolate – it should set within a few minutes and have a silky satiny texture.

TO DIP THE FONDANT FANCIES IN THE CHOCOLATE

12 Once the chocolate has been tempered, have a dampened J-cloth at hand, lightly wet your fingers with it and pick up one fondant fancy at a time (this will stop your fingers from sticking to the fondant) and dip the bottom into the chocolate until covered.

13 Place each on a wire rack for a few minutes to allow the excess chocolate to drip off and transfer it to a sheet of greaseproof paper to let it set.

14 Repeat for all the remaining fondant fancies.

TO FINISH

15 Put the remaining white icing into a paper piping bag and use it to stick the cherry blossoms randomly on top of the fondant fancies.

16 Store at room temperature for about 3-5 days.

**MAKES 4
MINI CAKES**

peggy's *Purses*

There is something about designer handbags that we girls simply can't resist. Although novelty cakes are not usually my thing, I couldn't help but wonder how my own signature purses would look if made from cake. They make wonderful birthday treats for a girlfriend and are surprisingly simple to make. Replace the monogram with a friend's initial to make it her own.

INGREDIENTS

one 20cm square Victoria sponge cake (this will hold the shape best), flavoured to your choice (page 114)
about 750g marzipan
about 150g buttercream, flavoured to your choice (page 120)
about 750g white sugar paste
dark-brown, dusky-pink (from Sugar Flair) and ivory (from Wilton) food paste colours
small amount of gum tragacanth
small amount of white vegetable fat
small amount of clear alcohol or edible glue
pearl lustre powder or spray
about 1 tablespoon royal icing (page 132)
small amount of water

EQUIPMENT

cake leveller
10cm round pastry cutter
small kitchen knife
small rolling pin
small palette knife
pair of cake smoothers
small bowls
palette knife
cling film
resealable plastic bag
design wheeler (from PME)
pastry brush
2 small round cutters (about 2cm and 3cm in diameter)
soft artist's brush (if using pearl lustre powder)
paper piping bags (page 134)

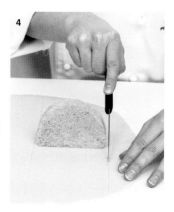

1 Trim the top and bottom crust of the sponge cake using the cake leveller. Your trimmed sponge should have a depth of about 4cm. Divide the cake into 4 even squares.

2 For the round bags, cut 3 semi-circles from 3 pieces of sponge (see 1). For the square handbag, cut the remaining sponge to a slightly oblong shape of about 7.5 x 8cm.

3 Stand the sponges upright and cut the wide sides at a slight angle to narrow them at the top (see 2 and 3).

4 For each cake, roll out a piece of marzipan about 11cm deep, 20cm wide and 3-4mm thick. Place a piece of sponge on one of these pieces and trim the marzipan to its width (see 4). Reserve trimmings.

5 Now lay the sponge on its side on top of the marzipan and cut it along the cake edge (see 4). Repeat for the other side; it should fit exactly.

6 To cover the top edge, cut some marzipan trimmings to fit (see 5).

7 Spread buttercream thinly along the top of the bag and place the marzipan on top. Trim the ends with a knife as they may have stretched.

8 Cover the bottom and sides of the sponge thinly with buttercream, centre it on top of the large cut piece of marzipan and wrap that around the sides (see 6).

9 Gently shape the cake sides using the cake smoothers (see 7). Repeat for the remaining purse cakes and let the marzipan firm up overnight.

10 Mix 300g sugar paste with dark-brown food colour to a chocolate colour, 300g with dusky-pink to a light pink, and the remaining 150g with a little ivory. To keep these fresh and soft, wrap in cling film or in a resealable bag until ready to use.

11 Mix about 50g each of the pale-pink sugar paste and the chocolate-brown paste with about ½ teaspoon of gum tragacanth and knead it with a small amount of white vegetable fat until smooth.

12 To cover the cakes with sugar paste, roll out pale pink, ivory and chocolate-brown paste to 3-4mm and large enough to cover the cakes.

13 Brush each cake with alcohol and cover with the required sugar paste colour by gently pushing down the sides with your hands (see 8). Trim off excess and polish with smoothers.

14 While the paste is still soft, for the brown and square pale-pink purses, run the stitching wheel of the design wheeler along the edges to emboss a stitched pattern.

TO DECORATE THE BROWN HANDBAG

15 Roll out more pale-pink paste and cut out a half-disc using the cutter used to cut out the sponge pieces, plus a small circle about 3cm in diameter for the monogram.

16 Brush the area that will be covered with the flap with a thin layer of alcohol or glue and stick the pale-pink half-disc of paste on top.

17 Repeat steps 15 and 16 (without making a smaller circle) to cover the pink flap with a slightly smaller flap made from the brown sugar paste and, after that, stick the smaller pink circle on top of the brown flap.

18 To make the pale-pink handles, roll the pale-pink sugar paste mixed

with the gum tragacanth until about 2mm thick and large enough to cut out 2 even strips about 1 x 6cm.

19 Trim the ends of both strips to a V-shape and curve them with your fingers. Let set for a couple of hours.

TO DECORATE THE IVORY HANDBAG

20 Roll out a long thin piece of the chocolate-brown paste mixed with the gum tragacanth and cut it into a thin strip about 4mm wide and long enough to fit around the base of the purse. Brush the base of the ivory purse with a thin layer of alcohol or glue and stick the strip around it.

21 Cut out another two 4cm long pieces for the handles and let dry in a curved shape for a couple of hours.

22 For the discs, roll a little pale-pink paste to 1mm thick and cut out 1–15 discs using the 2cm cutter. Brush the tops with pearl lustre.

23 Carefully brush the back of the dots with alcohol or glue and stick them across the sides of the ivory purse, trimming those that overlap with a knife to join the edges.

TO DECORATE THE PALE-PINK HALF-ROUND HANDBAG

24 Repeat steps 20 and 21, allowing extra paste to make more strips for the sides and the flap.

25 To make the bow, cut out 2 more strips that are slightly wider – about 7-8 mm wide and 6cm long.

26 Pinch one of the strips in the middle and at the ends, fold ends towards the centre and stick with a little glue. Cut a short piece off the second strip and wrap it around the centre of the bow; use a little glue to help it stick if necessary. Pinch the leftover strip of paste in the middle and bend it halfway over to a V-shape and trim the tails at an angle. (See also Hat Boxes, page 90, step 11.)

TO DECORATE THE PALE-PINK SQUARE PURSE

27 Make a chocolate-brown flap as in steps 15 and 16 (except for the making of the small circle).

28 Cover the base of the purse with a very thin strip made from the pale pink sugar paste mixed with gum tragacanth, as in step 20.

29 To make the bow, repeat steps 25 and 26 using pale-pink sugar paste mixed with gum tragacanth.

TO FINISH

30 Once all the handles are dry, divide the royal icing into 3 parts and colour them pale-pink, ivory and chocolate-brown. Add a little water for a soft-peak consistency (page 132).

31 Stick the handles on the purses with a dab of matching royal icing.

32 Using chocolate-brown icing, pipe a row of little dots around the pale-pink discs of the ivory purse. Then pipe the initial on the disc of the chocolate-brown purse, the tiny dots all over the sides of the pale-pink square bag and the little buttons on the handles of both pink bags.

33 Using the bag with the pale-pink icing, pipe the swag border along the edge of the brown flap for the square pale-pink bag as well as the buttons on the handles of the ivory and the chocolate-brown bags.

34 Stick the bows on to the pink bags using a little glue or icing.

**MAKES 12
CUP CAKES**

Cup Cakes
in bloom

These stunning hydrangea cup cakes will not fail to delight! Admittedly, I might have gone a little bit over the top, but when I started arranging the individual blossoms on top of the cup cakes I just couldn't resist adding more and more. I promise you that you will be showered with praise and hardly anyone will believe that the flowers are made of sugar, let alone that there is a cake underneath. Each cup cake is decorated with at least 15 hand-crafted blooms, making this design undoubtedly a labour of love.

INGREDIENTS

12 cup cakes, baked in silver metallic muffin cases, made from ½ recipe Victoria sponge (page 114), flavoured to your choice, soaked with syrup and iced with fondant icing to match the colours of the flowers: 2 soft-pink, 2 cerise-pink, 2 lilac, 2 lavender, 2 claret and 2 purple (page 131)

about 300g white sugar florist paste

small amount of white vegetable fat

burgundy and grape violet food colours (from Sugar Flair)

cornflour blue food colour (from Wilton)

burgundy, pink and purple edible dust colours (from Sugar Flair & Squires Kitchen)

about 3 tablespoons royal icing (page 132)

small amount of water

EQUIPMENT

small bowls

cling film or resealable plastic bags

small non-stick plastic board

small rolling pin

hydrangea flower cutter and petal veiner (from Sunflower Sugar Art)

piece of profile foam sheet (I get mine from a packaging supplier)

Stayfresh multi-mat

fine artist's brush

paper piping bags (page 134)

pair of scissors

small saucepan

MAKE THE HYDRANGEA BLOSSOMS AT LEAST ONE DAY IN ADVANCE

1 Knead the sugar florist paste with a small dab of white vegetable fat until soft and pliable and divide it into 6 equal parts.

2 Mix one part with the claret food colour to a soft-pink, a second with a little more claret food colour to a cerise-pink, a third with grape-violet food colour to a lilac, a fourth with a little more grape-violet to a purple, a fifth with a mixture of grape-violet and a tiny amount of cornflour-blue to a lavender and, finally, one with claret and grape-violet to a deep burgundy colour. Of course you can create your own shades and colour variations, but make sure that the colours of the flowers will match with the colours of the fondant icings. Always keep the paste you are not using covered in cling film to prevent it from drying out.

3 Lightly grease the non-stick plastic board with a small amount of white vegetable fat and roll one of the paste colours out to a thickness of 1mm.

4 For 2 cup cakes of the same colour, cut out about 30 hydrangea blossoms in total, using the hydrangea flower cutter.

5 Remove the excess paste from the plastic board and keep it covered in cling film or a resealable plastic bag to prevent it from drying out.

6 Take one blossom at a time and squeeze it between the 2 veining mats, then carefully remove it and place it inside a well of the profile foam sheet and let it dry. Repeat this process for the rest of the hydrangea blossoms and let them dry for at least 4 hours or ideally overnight. Keep the petals remaining on the board covered with the Stayfresh multi-mat to prevent them from drying out.

7 Once dry, dust the petal tips lightly with the dusting colours, using the fine artist's brush to create the natural shadings that are so characteristic of hydrangea. As all the colours work well together you can create your own variations; for example use the pink dust on the lavender blossoms, the burgundy on the purple blossoms and the purple dust on the pink blossoms. You can also mix the dust colours with each other to create even more different shades.

8 Once all the blossoms have been dusted, prepare one piping bag with soft-peak royal icing (page 132) to match each of the colours of the fondant icing and the flowers.

9 Snip a small tip off each bag and use it to stick the individual blossoms on top of the cup cakes and make sure that you are using the same colour of icing with that of the blossoms and the same colour of cup cake. Start by sticking the first blossom centred on the top and then arrange them all around row by row. Should you have any gaps, you can fill them by breaking off individual petals and sticking them into the gaps.

10 Put a small amount of water into a saucepan and bring it to the boil. As the steam is evaporating, hold each decorated cup cake over the steam for literally 2 seconds – this will bring the colours of the petal dust to life and make the hydrangea blooms look even more realistic. Be careful not to steam them for too long as this can melt the icing and burn your hands!

11 Once all the flowers have been steamed, pipe small dots of icing in a matching colour into all the blossom centres.

12 To store: keep these at room temperature for about 3-5 days.

**MAKES 12
CUP CAKES**

Dots and Bows

One of my most popular designs, this pretty and elegant cup cake is very easy to make and works wonderfully for almost any type of celebration. For weddings, why not try a white-on-white colour scheme, and, for a little girl's name day, pastel-pink and white look adorable.

INGREDIENTS

12 cup cakes made from ½ recipe quantity Victoria sponge, flavoured to choice, baked in silver muffin cases (page 114), soaked with syrup and iced with pale green fondant icing (page 131)
about 100g white sugar paste
about 100g white sugar florist paste
small amount of white vegetable fat
cornflour for dusting
small amount of edible glue
pearl lustre spray (from PME)
small amount of royal icing (page 132)
small amount of water

EQUIPMENT

small non-stick plastic board
small rolling pin
Stayfresh multi-mat
small kitchen knife
fine artist's brush
greaseproof or kitchen paper
paper piping bags (page 134)
small palette knife
cling film or resealable piping bag

1 Mix the sugar paste with the sugar florist paste and a small dab of white vegetable fat, and knead it until smooth and pliable.

2 On a plastic board lightly dusted with cornflour, roll out the paste until 2mm thick and cut it into 12 strips about 1.5cm wide and 10cm long.

3 Taking one strip at a time (keeping the rest covered), pinch it together in the middle and at both ends.

4 Brush the centre bit with a small amount of edible glue, fold both ends towards the middle and pinch them together. Repeat this process for all 12 bows.

5 To cover the bow centres, roll out some more paste to the same thickness as before and cut it into 12 strips each 1cm wide and 3cm long.

6 Taking one strip at a time (and keeping the rest covered), brush it with a thin layer of glue. Wrap one strip around the centre of each bow.

7 For the bow tails, roll out more paste and cut out 12 more strips to the same size as in step 2.

8 Taking one strip at a time (and keeping the rest covered), pinch it in the centre, then fold the tails over so that they are forming a V-shape and cut the ends off the strips at an angle.

9 Place all the bow pieces on a sheet of greaseproof paper and spray them with the pearl lustre spray to give them a satin shimmer.

10 While the tails are still soft, using the edible glue, stick them on top of the cup cakes with the tails towards the front, then stick on the bows centred on top.

11 Mix the royal icing with a small amount of water to a soft-peak consistency (page 132) and put it in a piping bag.

12 Snip a fine tip off the bag and pipe small dots all around the bows.

55
MINI CAKES

**MAKES 8
MINI CAKES**

Ice Crystal
cakes

Inspired by Victorian tree ornaments these beautifully ornate cakes are timelessly elegant and will add a touch of magic not only to your Christmas table but also to any winter-themed occasion. The symmetrical patterns are very easy to pipe in stages, simply by using the templates on page 141. If you prefer, you can also create your own patterns and just use my templates as a guide. To show how it's done, I have picked one cake as an example below. The technique of repeating and building up symmetrically piped patterns on top of one another is the same for all designs.

INGREDIENTS

eight 7.5cm round miniature cakes made from a 30cm square cake of your choice (pages 114-18), covered with marzipan and a mixture of ivory and pale blue sugar paste (pages 122-4)

pearl lustre spray (from PME)

about 2 tablespoons royal icing (page 132)

small amount of water

silver sugar pearls

white sugar sprinkles

EQUIPMENT

ice crystal templates (page 141)

greaseproof paper

scriber

small snowflake cutter (about 3cm diameter)

small palette knife

paper piping bags (page 134)

about 2.5m white gros grain ribbon, 15mm width

FOR ALL DESIGNS

1 Spray the pale-blue cakes with the pearl spray to give them an icy look.

2 Sketch the templates on to greaseproof paper, place them on top of the cakes and mark the icing with a scriber to guide you when piping the symmetrical designs directly on the cakes (see the illustrations on page 40).

FOR THE SAMPLE DESIGN FEATURED ON PAGE 57, TOP RIGHT-HAND CORNER

3 Emboss the middle of the cake with the snowflake cutter by gently pushing it down into the soft icing (see 1).

4 Mix about 1 tablespoon of royal icing with a small amount of water to a soft-peak consistency (page 132) and put it in a piping bag. Snip a small tip off the bag and begin by piping the outline of the snowflake and the straight lines and dots from the centre towards the edge of the cake (see 2).

5 Continue to pipe the scroll designs in between the lines and dots as shown below (see 3). Embellish with silver sugar pearls at this stage for the other designs where required.

6 Mix the remaining royal icing with a little more water to give a runny consistency (page 132), put it in a piping bag and use to flood the centre of the snowflake.

7 While the icing is still wet, sprinkle the white sugar sprinkles on top and let the icing dry (see 4).

8 Once dry, shake the excess sprinkles off the cake and stick a piece of ribbon around the base of the cake with a blob of royal icing.

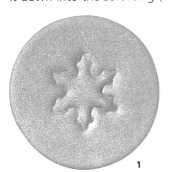

1

2

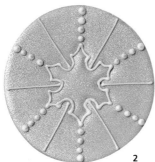

3

4

French fancies

My inspiration for these designs comes from an old French patisserie book I used to study during my training at Le Cordon Bleu. The piped chocolate designs have an appealing retro-feel and are easy to achieve with simple piping techniques. This type of fondant fancy is also known as a 'petit four', from the French for oven, and is traditionally layered with lots of very thin slices of sponge and butter cream. I used a wonderfully fragrant orange sponge with orange butter cream.

INGREDIENTS

16 Fondant Fancies dipped variously in pastel pink, yellow, blue, green and lilac fondant icing (page 129), made from a 20cm square Victoria sponge flavoured with orange zest (page 114) and filled with 3 layers of orange butter cream (page 120)
200g couverture chocolate buttons
1 tablespoon royal icing (page 132)
dark-brown food colour (I use paste colour from Sugar Flair)
small amount of water

EQUIPMENT

small microwaveable bowl
microwave cooker
digital thermometer
small palette knife
J-cloth
wire rack
greaseproof paper
paper piping bag (page 134)
pair of scissors

TO TEMPER THE CHOCOLATE

1 Place 150g of the chocolate buttons in a microwaveable bowl and melt it gently on medium heat. Be careful not to overheat it as chocolate can burn easily. Check the temperature with a thermometer; it should be melted and between 44 and 48°C.

2 Once it has reached the required temperature, stir the remaining chocolate buttons into the melted chocolate and this will cool it down to 28°C.

3 Once the chocolate has cooled down to 28°C, gently warm it up again to between 32 and 34°C. The chocolate should now be tempered. You can test it by dipping a palette knife into it – it should set on the blade within a few minutes and have a silky satiny texture.

TO DIP THE FONDANT FANCIES IN THE CHOCOLATE

4 Once the chocolate has been tempered, have a dampened J-cloth at hand, slightly wet your fingers with it and pick up one fondant fancy at a time (this will stop your fingers from sticking to the fondant) and dip the bottom into the chocolate until well covered.

5 Place each on a wire rack for a few minutes to allow excess chocolate to drip off and then transfer it to a sheet of greaseproof paper to let it set.

TO FINISH

6 Mix the royal icing with the dark-brown food colour and a bit of water to a soft-peak consistency (page 132). Put it into a piping bag.

7 Snip a small tip off the bag and pipe the different designs directly on to the fondant fancies.

8 To store: keep at room temperature for about 3-5 days.

Large Cakes

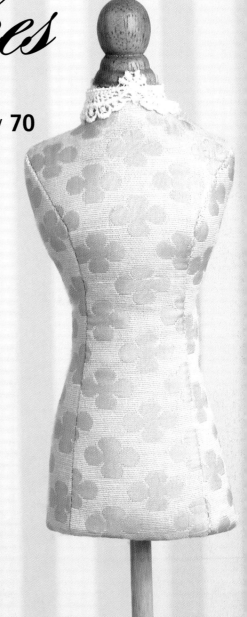

pure *White* perfection

The inspiration for this cake, perhaps obviously, came from a wedding dress. The flowers are so simple to make and yet they are so effective. Their sheer abundance is complemented by piped swirls which give a very sophisticated feel. This cake would be perfect for a special birthday or anniversary party.

INGREDIENTS

15cm diameter round cake, flavoured to your choice (see pages 114-121), iced with 600g marzipan and 600g white sugar paste

about 250g white sugar florist paste

small amount of white vegetable fat

pearl lustre spray (PME) or pearl lustre powder (Sugar Flair)

about 300g royal icing (page 132)

EQUIPMENT

3 small circle cutters, ranging in diameter from 1cm to 2cm

small rolling pin

small non-stick plastic board

Stayfresh multi-mat

bulbous cone or frilling tool

soft artist's brush (if using lustre powder)

20cm round cake board covered with 600g white sugar paste (see page 127)

about 1.2 metres white satin ribbon 15mm width

pair of scissors

small plastic bowl

small palette knife

paper piping bags (see page 134)

tiltable turntable (PME)

TO MAKE THE FLOWERS

1 The cake uses 3 different sizes of 5-petal flowers and you will need about 10 in each size. To make the individual petals, use circular cutters in 3 different sizes ranging from 1cm to 2 cm.

2 Roll a small amount of white sugar florist's paste out on a plastic board, lightly greased with the fat, to a thickness of about 1mm.

3 Cut out about 5-6 petals in each size at a time (see 1) and keep the remaining paste covered with the Stayfresh multi-mat to prevent it from drying out.

4 Now roll each individual petal out again using the bulbous cone or frilling tool until it is so thin that you can almost see through it, but still ensuring that it will keep its shape (see 2). Now that the petal is very thin, pinch it together at the bottom and gather it slightly to produce the ruching effect (see 3). Let dry briefly.

5 After you have made 5 petals, it helps to lay them together to check that the sizes all match, before you move on to the next flower. Repeat for the remaining petals using the appropriate cutter sizes.

6 To make the leaves, use the medium-sized circle cutter and roll out petal shapes as before.

7 To shape the leaves, fold over the two sides at the top half of the circle to a tip and pinch lightly. Gather and pinch the paste together at the bottom to a leaf shape (see 4).

8 For the flower centres, shape small balls of paste about 5mm in diameter.

9 Spray all the flower petals, leaves and flower centres evenly with pearl lustre spray. Or, you can brush them individually with lustre powder, but it will take much longer (see 5).

TO ASSEMBLE AND FINISH

10 Spread a small amount of royal icing in the middle of the iced cake board and then place the cake on top.

11 Secure the white ribbon around the base of the cake and around the edge of the iced cake board with blobs of royal icing.

12 In a small bowl, mix the remaining royal icing with a little water to soft-peak consistency (see page 132) and fill into a piping bag.

13 Snip a small tip off the piping bag and pipe a row of fine dots around the ribbon edges at 1cm intervals.

14 Place the cake on the turntable and tilt it slightly away from you. Start decorating it by piping swirls all around the sides and the top.

15 Finally, stick on the flowers and leaves using royal icing (see 6).

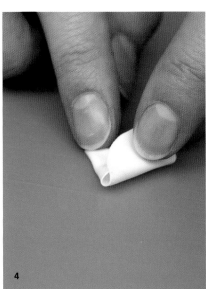

MAKES ABOUT 170 FINGER-SIZED PORTIONS
OR 75 DESSERT PORTIONS

Summer symphony

Inspired by Neapolitan ice cream, I designed this cake for a summer wedding, but it suits any summer party. The decoration is fairly simple, so it is a relatively easy cake to make for larger numbers. To match the design it has layers of vanilla, pistachio, strawberry and chocolate filling.

INGREDIENTS

10cm round cake made from ¼ recipe quantity vanilla Victoria sponge, soaked with vanilla syrup (page 114), layered with vanilla, chocolate and strawberry buttercream, and covered with 400g each marzipan and pastel-pink sugar paste (pages 125-6)

15cm round cake made from ½ recipe quantity Victoria sponge, flavoured, soaked and layered as above, covered with 600g each marzipan and pistachio-coloured sugar paste

20cm round cake made from 1 recipe quantity Victoria sponge, flavoured, soaked and layered as above, and covered with 850g each marzipan and ivory-coloured sugar paste

25cm square cake made from 2 recipe quantities Victoria sponge, flavoured, soaked and layered as above, and covered with 1.25kg each marzipan and pistachio-coloured sugar paste

about 500g royal icing (page 132)

ivory, pink and moss-green food colours

about 250g sugar paste

small amount of gum tragacanth

small amount of white vegetable fat

edible glue or alcohol

EQUIPMENT

12 plastic dowels

32.5cm square cake board, covered with 950g pastel-pink sugar paste (page 125-6)

20cm cake board for use as a template

several paper piping bags (page 134)

1.2m ivory satin ribbon, 7mm width

tilting turntable

small rolling pin

icing sugar for dusting

small lattice–impression rolling pin

round pastry cutter (about 3.5cm)

small round pastry cutter (about 5mm)

1.2m Neapolitan stripes ribbon, 25mm width;1.5m Neapolitan stripes ribbon, 35mm width

1.3m pastel-pink satin ribbon, 15mm width; 50cm pastel-pink satin ribbon, 7mm width

70
LARGE CAKES

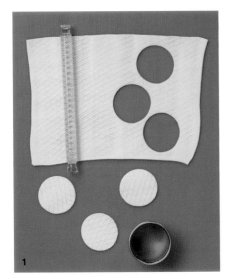

1 Using the template on page 144, mark positions for dowels on all but the smallest cake. Push 4 dowels into place on each of the 3 cakes as described on page 128.

2 Spread a thin layer of icing in the middle of the iced cake board and place the 25cm square tier on it.

3 Now spread a little icing in the middle of the top of the 25cm tier and place the 20cm ivory tier on top. Let set for about half an hour.

4 While it dries, using the 20cm cake board as a guide, centred on top of the second tier, scratch a circle. Then poke tiny holes along this line at about 1cm intervals. This will indicate where to pipe stripes.

5 Prepare piping bags for piping the stripes: one with pastel-pink and another with pistachio-green soft-peak royal icing (page 132).

6 Place the ivory ribbon around the base of the second tier and stick down the ends with icing at the back.

7 Place the stacked tiers on the turntable and slightly tilt away from you. Pipe green lines down the side, starting at the little holes and moving the bag straight down to the bottom, finishing with a small dot (see 3).

8 Pipe a pastel-pink stripe in between every other green one, finishing in the same way with a small dot at the base. Let dry.

9 For the third tier, mix about 200g sugar paste with a little ivory colour and a little gum tragacanth (to make it more flexible). Place the paste on a lightly greased plastic board and roll out about 2mm thick.

10 For the wafer-effect pattern, roll over the paste once with the lattice-embossed rolling pin, keeping the pressure the same at all times.

11 Using the larger cutter, cut out discs (see 1) and stick them evenly around the cake, using edible glue. Put the third tier in place on top of the second, fixing it with icing.

12 For the top tier, divide the remaining sugar paste into 3, keep one ivory and mix the other two with pink food colour to make one light pink and the other dark pink.

13 Roll all colours of paste out to about 1mm thick and cut out little dots using the smaller circle cutter (see 2). Stick randomly all over the top tier, using glue or clear alcohol.

14 Place the narrow Neapolitan ribbon around the base of the bottom tier and secure with icing. Do the same with the wider pastel-pink ribbon on the cake board.

15 Put the top tier in position on the third tier, securing it with royal icing. Place the narrower pastel-pink ribbon around the base of the top tier, sticking it in place with icing.

16 Tie the wider Neapolitan ribbon into a bow and, using icing, stick it on the side of the top tier, resting on the third tier. Snip the ribbon tails in a 'v'-shape.

pink Poodle cake

Fun and flirtatious, this cake provides the perfect opportunity to send a message of love! It's not just a great design for a loved one's birthday, for simply by rewording the message you could also turn it into a great gift for a couple's wedding anniversary or engagement party.

INGREDIENTS

3 square cake tiers of 10, 15 and 20cm, made of a cake and filling of your choice (pages 114-21), covered with marzipan and ivory sugar paste (page 125-6), stacked and assembled on a 30cm square cake board (pages 128-9)
about 400g royal icing (page 132)
claret and black food paste colours
small amount of white vegetable fat
about 300g white sugar florist paste
small amount of edible glue

EQUIPMENT

palette knife
small bowls
sheet of acetate or plastic sleeve
poodle and Eiffel Tower templates (page 144)
cling-film or resealable plastic bag
small non-stick plastic board
greaseproof paper
small plastic rolling pin
small kitchen knife
artist's brush
pair of scissors
selection of small heart-shaped cutters
about 3.5m black-and-white micro-dot satin ribbon, 15mm width
small piece of double-sided sticky tape

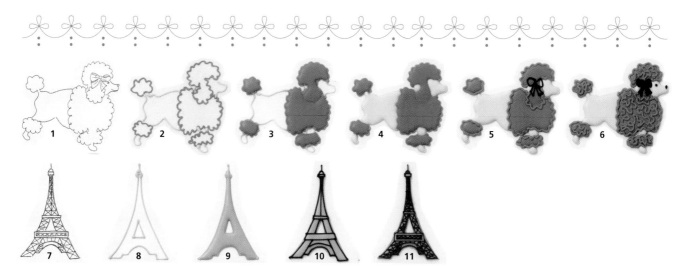

1　2　3　4　5　6

7　8　9　10　11

MAKE THE BOW AND THE RUN-OUTS A DAY AHEAD

FOR THE RUN-OUTS

1 Prepare your piping bags; you will need:

1 bag each soft-peak (page 132) bright-pink royal icing (made from claret food colour) and runny bright-pink icing

1 bag each soft-peak pale-pink royal icing (made from claret food colour) and runny pale pink icing

1 bag each grey soft-peak royal icing (made from black food colour) and runny grey icing

1 bag each black soft-peak royal icing and black runny icing

2 Rub a very thin layer of vegetable fat over the acetate or plastic sleeve. Lay it on top of the poodle template (see 1) and pipe the outlines using soft-peak pale-pink and grey royal icing for the bodies and bright pink and black for the hair (see 2).

3 Flood the centres of the hairy sections with the coordinating runny icing colours (see 3) and let them dry a little. Once the icing is beginning to set you can flood the bodies with the coordinating icing colours (see 4). Let dry overnight.

4 For the Eiffel Tower, outline the shape (see 7) with the soft-peak grey icing (see 8) and flood it with the same colour of runny icing (see 9). Let it dry overnight.

5 Once the run-outs have dried completely, pipe the details of the hair, the bows and faces of the poodles and the Eiffel Tower structures, using the soft-peak royal icing colours accordingly (see 5, 6, 10 and 11). Let dry completely.

FOR THE BOW

6 Mix the sugar florist paste with the claret food colour and a small amount of white vegetable fat to a bright-pink smooth and pliable paste. Keep it covered with cling-film or inside a resealable plastic bag to prevent it from drying out.

7 Take about half of the paste and roll it out on a slightly greased non-stick plastic board to about 2mm thick, 10cm wide and 25cm long.

8 Trim the edges with a knife and fold each side of the paste horizontally towards the middle (see left). Pinch the strip of paste together in the middle as well as on both ends. Brush a small amount of edible glue into the middle of the paste, fold both ends over and pinch them down in the centre.

9 For the middle part of the bow, roll out a smaller piece of paste to the same thickness as before and about 4cm wide by 8cm long. Fold it as before and pinch both ends together.

10 Brush a thin layer of edible glue on both ends and wrap the strip around the middle of the bow. Let the bow dry and keep the leftover pink paste wrapped until the next day.

TO APPLY THE DECORATIONS ON THE FOLLOWING DAY

11 Use the soft-peak black icing to pipe your inscription on the front of the middle tier. If you have good practice in piping free-hand, then use your own free-hand style. However, should you be a bit nervous about it, then simply first trace the message on to greaseproof paper and, using it as a template, scratch it into the icing with a scriber needle. If you tilt the cake away from you slightly, it is easier to follow the marks with your piping bag.

12 Cut the ribbon into 4 pieces long enough to fit around the individual tiers and the cake board. Stick the ribbon around the cake tiers with dabs of royal icing, and the ribbon on the board with double-sided sticky tape.

13 Using a palette knife and first making sure they are completely dry, carefully lift the poodle and Eiffel Tower run-outs off the acetate or plastic sleeve. Using a little royal icing, stick the poodles on the front of the bottom tier, facing each other, and the Eiffel Tower on the top tier.

14 Before sticking the bow on top of the cake, make the bow tails by repeating step 8. Once folded, cut the strip of paste in half and pinch each tail on one end, and cut it at an angle on the other end (see left).

15 Brush the middle of the top tier and the two front corners with

edible glue and stick the tails on so that they are falling over the corners towards the front of the cake.

16 Now stick the bow on top, where the tails join, securing it with edible glue.

17 Roll the leftover pink paste out to about 1mm thick and cut out little heart shapes. Stick them all over the cake as shown.

**MAKES ABOUT 20
FINGER-SIZED PORTIONS
OR 10 DESSERT PORTIONS**

Anemone
cake

Anemones look great for any vintage-themed party, be it a birthday, a mother's day lunch or a wedding. The original idea for this design comes from a cake I created for the style pages of *Wedding Magazine*. The black-and-cream colour combination is very contemporary, yet the frilly petals with a hint of dusky pink add a touch of romance.

INGREDIENTS

One 15cm round cake with flavour and filling of your choice (pages 114-21), covered with marzipan and ivory sugar paste (page 125-6) on an ivory-iced 20cm round cake board (page 127)

about 150g white sugar florist paste

ivory and black food colour pastes

small amount of white vegetable fat

small amount of cornflour for dusting

small amount of black sprinkling sugar (I got mine from a sugar craft shop)

dusky-pink blossom tint

small amount of royal icing (page 132)

EQUIPMENT

small non-stick plastic board

small rolling pin

anemone petal cutters (small, medium and large)

flower foam pad

Stayfresh multi-mat

ball tool

veining tool

plastic paint palette

edible glue

fine artist's brush

cling-film or resealable plastic bag

small scissors

black flower stamens

paper piping bags (page 135)

50cm black-and-white microdot ribbon, 25mm width

65cm black-and-white microdot ribbon, 15mm width

double-sided sticky tape

50cm cream-coloured satin ribbon, 25mm width

black and roll into 2 hazelnut-sized balls and one slightly smaller.

8 While the balls are still soft, cut the black stamens to about 1.25cm (see 6), dip the bottom part into the glue and push them into the sides of the balls to create an even ring of stamens around each ball (see 7).

9 Brush the tops of the black balls with edible glue and dip them upside down into the black sprinkling sugar to give them a bit of texture (see 8).

10 Now stick each flower centre into the middle of each anemone using a small amount of edible glue and let it dry completely.

11 Once dry, brush the petal tips of the anemones with the dusky-pink blossom tint (see 9).

12 Prepare 2 bags of royal icing; one filled with ivory stiff-peak (page 132), and the other black soft-peak.

13 Arrange the cream satin ribbon around the base of the cake and stick it with ivory icing, followed by the 25mm black-and-white ribbon. Tie a little bow out of the remaining black-and-white 25mm ribbon and stick it on the side of the cake with the double-sided sticky tape. Then arrange the 15mm ribbon around the cake board and fix it with the double-sided sticky tape.

14 Pipe small dots evenly all over the cake using black icing. Stick the anemones in a cluster on the edge of the cake using the ivory icing.

1 Mix 125g white sugar florist paste with a small amount of ivory food colour and a dab of white vegetable fat to a smooth and pliable paste.

2 On a lightly greased plastic board, roll the paste about 1-2mm thick. Cut out petal shapes using the anemone petal cutters (see 1): for the 2 large flowers you need 4 large and 4 medium petals each; for the small flower 4 medium and 4 small petals.

3 Place a couple of petals on the flower foam pad at a time, keeping the others covered with the multi-mat. Flatten each petal with the ball tool and slightly frill the edges (see 2).

4 Roll the veining tool lengthwise across each petal to emboss the veins (see 3). Once all the petals are shaped, let them set slightly inside the wells of the paint palette.

5 Once feeling slightly rubbery, stick together the 4 larger petals, using a small amount of edible glue at the bottom tips, and place inside a well of the palette that has been lightly dusted with cornflour (see 4 and 5).

6 Stick the 4 smaller petals on top of the large using the edible glue.

7 To make the flower centres, mix the remaining white sugar florist paste to

Mochaccino dots

This is a simple but smart idea for a truly scrumptious dessert cake to have with a cup of coffee! The polka dots don't just look fun and are easy to make, but they are also very helpful when dividing the cake into perfect portions – one dot for a cocktail-sized party portion, two dots for dessert.

INGREDIENTS

1 rich dark chocolate cake baked one day in advance (pages 115-6) in a rectangular baking tray about 30 x 37.5cm (you can use a smaller tray that fits your oven)
200g vanilla buttercream (page 120)
400g mocha buttercream (page 120)
about 200g ganache (page 121)
about 500g chocolate covering paste
about 300g ivory sugar paste
dark-brown food paste colour
icing sugar for dusting
small amount of clear alcohol or edible glue

EQUIPMENT

cake leveller
palette knife
kitchen knife
pastry brush
rolling pin
round pastry cutter (about 4cm)
cling-film
microwave cooker

1 Cut the chocolate sponge horizontally into half and trim the top and bottom crusts using the cake leveller. Slice each piece into 2 even layers using the cake leveller.

2 Sandwich the four layers together with alternating layers of mocha and vanilla buttercream.

3 Once all the layers have been stacked together, wrap the cake in cling-film and chill until it has set and feels firm. This could take a few hours, depending on your fridge.

4 Once the cake has set, prepare your chocolate covering paste. It is usually very hard when cold and needs warming up in the microwave cooker at medium heat to soften it.

5 Once softened, knead it until pliable and, on a flat surface dusted with icing sugar, roll it out to a thickness of about 3mm and large enough to cover the top of the cake.

6 Remove the cake from the fridge and spread the top with a very thin layer of ganache to help the paste stick to the top. Place the sheet of paste on top and trim off excess.

7 Use a sharp knife, trim a thin slice off all the sides of the cake to give it a perfect clean shape.

8 Divide the ivory sugar paste into 3 portions and mix each one with a different small amount of the leftover chocolate covering paste until you end up with one café latte, one caramel and one mocha-coloured piece of paste.

9 On a flat surface dusted with icing sugar, roll each piece of paste out to about 2mm thick and cut out enough discs to cover the top of the cake.

10 To stick them on, brush the back of each with a small amount of clear alcohol or edible glue and arrange in rows, alternating the colours.

**MAKES ABOUT 90 FINGER-SIZED
OR 40 DESSERT PORTIONS**

couture *Hat Boxes*

Ever since I moved to London and discovered Lulu Guinness's fabulous designs, I have been fascinated by hat boxes, in particular stripy ones with pretty bows. I thought these could be a fun and quirky idea for a girly birthday cake and a rather more special alternative to a gift box cake.

INGREDIENTS

two 15cm hexagonal cakes with the filling of your choice (page 113-18), covered with marzipan and one with lilac sugar paste and the other with dusky-pink sugar paste (pages 125-6, the portions needed for a hexagonal cake work out to be much the same as for a round cake)

one 23cm hexagonal cake with the filling of your choice, covered with marzipan and purple sugar paste

about 200g white sugar paste

about 300g white sugar florist paste

small amount of white vegetable fat

purple, dusky-pink and ivory food paste colour

edible glue

iced coffee lustre dust (from Edable Art)

small amount of royal icing (page 132)

EQUIPMENT

small non-stick plastic board

small rolling pin

cling-film or resealable plastic bag

small kitchen knife

Stayfresh multi-mat

fine artist's brush

4 plastic dowels

serrated knife

dowels template (page 144)

marker pen

design wheeler (from PME)

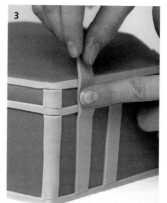

1 Mix the sugar paste and the sugar florist paste together with a small amount of the vegetable fat to make it smooth and pliable.

TIP: To create a soft and smooth modelling paste, I mix sugar paste with sugar florist paste. The ratio required depends on how strong it needs to be – the more sugar florist paste, the stronger the paste. In general I use a ratio of equal parts of each or up to two-thirds sugar florist paste to one-third sugar paste.

2 Divide the mixed paste into 4 equal pieces. Mix one with the purple food colour to a deep-purple shade and one to a lilac, then mix one to a dusky-pink shade and one to a dark-cream colour using the ivory food colour. Store wrapped in cling film or a resealable plastic bag to prevent them from drying out.

DECORATE ALL CAKE TIERS WITH STRIPS:
3 To make the strips for the purple cake, take the dusky-pink paste and roll it out on the non-stick plastic board until about 1mm thick. Cut out thin strips about 4-5mm wide

and stick them around the bottom and top edge with edible glue. Place another strip about 1.25cm below and parallel to the strip at the top. If your strips are not long enough to go all around the cakes, join them on the corners.

4 Now roll out another piece of paste and cut out more strips about 1.25cm wide and long enough to cover the depth of the cake (see 1). Keep them covered with the multi-mat so that they don't dry out.

5 Brush the area of cake that will be covered with paste with edible glue (see 2) and place the sugar paste strip on top (see 3). Trim overlapping paste with a knife (see 4).

6 Continue to arrange the strips all around the sides of the cake with even gaps in between. Then do the same for the top of the cake.

7 Repeat steps 3 to 6 for the 2 other cake tiers using the purple paste to make the strips for the lilac cake, and the lilac paste to make the strips for the dusky pink cake. Let dry until the strips have hardened.

STACKING THE 2-TIER CAKE:
8 Dowel the 23cm bottom tier as described on pages 128-9 and stick the 15cm lilac cake with the purple strips on top of it with royal icing.

MAKING THE BOWS:
9 For the bow of the large cake, roll the cream-colour paste out to about 2mm thick and cut it into strips about 2.5cm wide and 12.5cm long. Mark/emboss a stitched design along both sides of each strip using the design wheeler (see 5). Brush the strips with the iced coffee lustre (see 6).

10 Turn one of the strips upside down and pinch the paste together in the middle. Then fold both ends towards the middle and pinch them together using a small amount of edible glue to hold them in place (see 7).

11 Take another strip of the paste for the tails and fold them over in the middle so that both tails are facing to one side in a V-shape; cut the tails at an angle with a knife (see 8).

12 Cut a 4cm long piece off the remaining strip of paste and wrap it around the middle of the bow using a little edible glue to stick it on.

13 Repeat steps 9 to 12 for the 2 remaining smaller bows, cutting the strips of paste slightly thinner and shorter than before.

14 Let the bows and tails set a little bit and, once they feel slightly rubbery, stick them on the front of each cake with edible glue.

15 For the handles, roll the rest of the cream-colour paste out to the same thickness as before and as long as possible. Cut it into three 5mm wide strips and emboss each with a stitching design along the centre using the design wheeler. Brush with iced coffee pearl lustre.

16 Shape 12 small balls from the trimmings of the cream paste and brush them with the lustre as well.

17 Using the edible glue, attach the box handles to the sides of each of the boxes and arrange them on top of each tier. Place a cream paste ball at the ends of each handle.

**MAKES ABOUT 50 FINGER-SIZED PORTIONS
OR 25 DESSERT PORTIONS**

coco's *Corsage*

My inspiration here comes from the undisputed doyenne of haute couture Coco Chanel. The lattice design is iconic for so many of her creations and the colour combination of navy, cream and pearl is simply timeless and elegant. This cake suits any sophisticated wedding or other occasion.

INGREDIENTS

2 round cake tiers, 20cm and 12.5cm, flavoured to your choice (pages 114-21), freshly iced with marzipan and ivory sugar paste (pages 125-6)

pearl spray or lustre dust

small quantity of royal icing (page 132)

EQUIPMENT

turntable (optional)

ruler

scriber

design wheeler with stitching attachment

4 plastic dowels

serrated knife

small palette knife

3m navy-blue satin ribbon, 50mm width

pair of scissors

double-sided sticky tape

pearl diamante brooch

5-6 medium-sized cream-colour roses (not treated with pesticides)

1 While the icing is still soft, using a ruler and a scriber, mark the sides of each tier with a row of dots around the top edge spaced about 2.5cm apart, then repeat this around the middle of each tier and around the bottom, making sure the dots all line up underneath each other (see 1).

2 Using the dots as a spacing guide, emboss a diagonal lattice design with the design wheeler all around the sides of each of the tiers (see 2 and 3).

3 Spray the icing all over with a light dusting of pearl shimmer.

4 Dowel the bottom tier as described on pages 128-9 and stick the smaller tier on top with royal icing.

5 Cut the ribbon to fit around the base of the bottom and top tiers, and stick in place with dabs of icing.

6 Tie a bow out of the remaining piece of ribbon, attach the brooch in the middle of the bow and stick on to the ribbon at the front of the top tier with double-sided tape.

7 Arrange the rose heads on top of the cake and sprinkle a few petals around the cake table.

Button
flowers cake

This cool cake for crafty chicks and domestic goddesses was inspired by a button flower brooch. The cake design is daringly different, almost whimsical and frivolous.

INGREDIENTS

two 6cm deep cakes, one 10cm square and one 20cm square, flavoured and filled to your choice (pages 114-21), covered with marzipan and ecru sugar paste (pages 125-6)

one 10cm deep, 15cm square cake, flavoured and filled to your choice, covered with marzipan and peach-coloured sugar paste

one 10cm deep, 25cm square cake, flavoured and filled to your choice, covered with marzipan and soft-pink-coloured sugar paste

all assembled (pages 128-9) on a 30cm square cake board covered with ecru icing (page 127)

about 400g white sugar florist paste

small amount of white vegetable fat

ivory, pink, peach and dark brown food colour

pearl spray (from PME)

iced coffee lustre (Edable Art)

small amount of edible glue

small amount of royal icing

small amount of water

EQUIPMENT

cling-film or resealable plastic bag

small non-stick plastic board

small rolling pin

3 round cutters (about 6, 15 and 20mm diameter)

scriber

ordinary rolling pin

linen-look roller (Holly Products)

6-petal pastry cutter (about 8cm diameter)

petunia cutter (medium size)

bridal lily cutter (FMM)

fine artist's brush

soft artist's brush for dusting

small and medium arum lily petal cutter or other simple leaf cutter

small 5-petal cutter (25mm diameter)

flower foam pad

bone tool

about 3m ecru-coloured ribbon with stitched edges, 10mm width

paper piping bags (page 134)

small palette knife

about 1.2 ecru-coloured satin ribbon, 15mm width

1 Mix the sugar florist paste with a small amount of white vegetable fat until smooth and pliable.

2 Divide the paste into 4 equal quantities and mix one to an ivory, one to a soft-pink, one to a peach and one to an ecru (using a small amount of dark-brown) shade. Keep them covered with cling-film or inside a resealable plastic bag to prevent the pastes from drying out.

MAKE THE BUTTONS: YOU WILL NEED ABOUT 1 ECRU, 32 IVORY, 32 PEACH AND 22 PALE-PINK BUTTONS IN TOTAL.

3 Taking one colour of paste at a time, roll a small piece of it out until it is about 1-2mm thin.

4 Using the 20mm round cutter, stamp out the button shapes. Then use the 15mm round cutter to emboss the button edge (see 1).

5 Make 4 little holes in the centre of the buttons using the scriber (see 1) and let it dry. Repeat for all the remaining buttons.

6 Once the buttons are made, spray them with the pearl spray to make them shiny.

MAKE THE BUTTONS FLOWERS:

7 Using a normal rolling pin, roll out the ivory sugar paste until about 2-3mm thick.

8 Emboss the linen texture into the paste by rolling the linen-look roller once across it using an even pressure.

9 Using the 6-petal cutter, cut out 2 large 6-petal flower shapes (see 2).

10 Re-roll the ivory paste, using the plain rolling pin, to about 1mm thick and use the petunia cutter to cut out 3 petunia shapes (see 6).

11 Now roll out the pale-pink paste to the same thickness as before and use the bridal lily cutter to cut out a pale-pink lily flower shape. Repeat for the peach lily flower shape using the peach-coloured paste. Emboss each one with a polka dot pattern using the 6mm round cutter (see 3).

12 Roll out the ecru colour paste and cut out 2 more lily flower shapes (see 4). Brush them with the iced coffee lustre for a light shimmer and cut out polka dots using the 6mm round cutter at the same positions of the petals as you

embossed the pale-pink and peach lily flowers. This will ensure that the dots match perfectly with the edges of the flower petals.

13 Using a fine artist's brush with some edible glue, stick the shimmered dots on the matching embossed dots of the petals of the pale-pink and peach lily flowers.

14 Re-roll the remaining ecru paste and cut out 4 medium and 2 small arum lily petals (or leaves if using leaf cutters) and pinch them to form leaf shapes. Brush with the iced coffee pearl lustre (see 5).

15 To make small 5-petal flower shapes, roll out the peach-coloured paste and cut out 2 blossoms. Place on a flower foam pad and slightly stretch each petal with the bone tool (see 7).

16 To assemble the 2 large button flowers, stick the flower shapes on top of each other in the following order, starting with the largest flower on the bottom:
    6-petal linen-textured flowers
    pink or peach spotty lily flower

ivory petunia flower
small peach 5-petal flower (for the
one with the pink spotty lily only)
2 buttons (1 ecru / 1 pink)
For the smaller flower, from the bottom:
ivory petunia flower
small peach 5-petal flower
pink button.
Let the flowers and leaves dry.

17 Mix a small amount of royal icing with the dark-brown food colour and a small amount of water to an ecru colour soft-peak royal icing consistency (page 132).

18 Arrange the stitched ribbon around the base of each tier and hold in place with dabs of icing. Arrange the plain ribbon around the cake board in the same way.

19 Stick the buttons on top of the ribbons with icing, using the ivory ones for the ecru cake tiers, the pink buttons for the peach tier and the peach buttons for the pink cake tier.

20 Once flowers and leaves are dry, stick them on the cake with icing.

21 Pipe little crosses into the middle of each button to look like threads.

Tiffany pearls

Diamonds may be most girls' best friends, but mine are pearls! And just as much as I like wearing them, I think they look exquisite if iced on to a cake. The piped pearl designs of this cake require a very simple technique, yet they transform a simple cake into a glamorous yet understated centrepiece. The individual pearl designs are all inspired by different pieces of jewellery – the band of pearls around the shorter tiers reminds me of a choker, the tear droplets of the third tier are taken from a beautiful pair of earrings and the drapes of the bottom tier originate from a pearl necklace my mum gave to me when I got married.

INGREDIENTS

2 round cakes tiers about 10cm deep, one 25cm and the other 15cm in diameter

2 round cake tiers about 6cm deep, one 20cm and the other 10cm in diameter

All four made of the cake and filling of your choice (pages 114-21), iced with marzipan and pale-blue sugar paste (page 125-6) with the bottom to the third tier already doweled (pages 127-8)

32.5cm round cake board also iced with pale-blue sugar paste (page 127)

about 300g royal icing (page 132)

ivory food paste colour

small amount of water

small amount of piping gel

pearl lustre

EQUIPMENT

side scribing/marking gauge (from Kitbox)

ruler

scriber

small palette knife

paper piping bag (page 134)

turntable

fine artist's brush

scissors

about 2.5m bridal white satin ribbon, 7mm width, and 1.1m at 15mm width

double-sided sticky tape

1

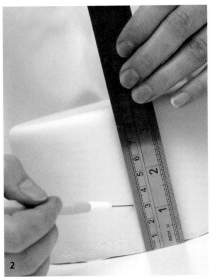

2

3

MARK THE TIERS BEFORE PIPING THE PEARL DESIGNS

1 For the second and top tier, using the side scribing/marking gauge, scribe 3 parallel lines centred along the sides of each tier, spacing them about 1cm apart.

2 For the third tier, scribe a line around the side about 2.5cm down from the top edge of the cake (see 1) and divide the line into 12 even sections, marking them with the scriber. Now mark the positions for the tear droplets about 5cm down from each section and again mark them using the ruler and scriber (see 2).

3 For the bottom tier, divide the top edge into 8 even sections and mark with the scriber.

Now place a ruler centred between each section and mark it at about 3.75cm down from the top edge and another 2 further down the cake spacing them 1.25cm apart. These will indicate the lowest points of each of the swags.

PIPE THE PEARL DESIGNS

4 Spread a thin layer of royal icing on the iced cake board and place the bottom tier on top.

5 Mix the remaining royal icing with a little bit of ivory food colour and water to a soft-peak (page 132) off-white colour. Put it in a piping bag and snip a small tip off the point.

6 One by one, place each tier on top of a turntable and pipe the pearls, droplets and swag designs

around the sides, using the lines and markings as a guide. Let dry.

7 Once dry, mix a small amount of piping gel with a bit of pearl lustre to a thick paste and, using the artist's brush, paint the pearls with the lustre to make them shiny (see 3).

8 Stack the tiers on top of one another as described on pages 128-9 and arrange the 7mm ribbon around the sides of each tier and fix them with a dab of royal icing.

9 Arrange the 15mm ribbon around the board and stick it down with double-sided sticky tape.

Basics

basic equipment

1 large rolling pin
2 small non-stick plastic board
3 flower foam pad
4 marzipan spacers
5 design wheeler
6 artists' paint brushes
7 frilling or bulbous cone tool
8 ruler
9 scissors
10 dowelling template
11 small kitchen knife
12 small and large palette knife
13 large serrated kitchen knife
14 round pastry cutters
15 wire cooling rack
16 assortment of cake boards
17 whisk
18 rubber spatula
19 plastic sleeves
20 pastry brush
21 greaseproof paper
22 cake tins
23 selection of food colours
24 muffin cases
25 paper piping bag
26 muffin tray
27 baking tray
28 metal top and side scraper
29 veining tool
30 truffle dipping fork
31 bone tool
32 scriber needle
33 ball tool
34 cutting wheel
35 small rolling pin
36 cake leveller
37 assortment of cookie cutters
38 plastic dowels
39 mixing bowl/electric mixer with paddle attachment
40 assorted ribbons
41 rubber cameo moulds
42 sugar pearls
43 profile foam sheet
44 small painter's palette
45 selection of sprinkling sugars
46 cake smoothers
47 flower cutter and veiner

food *Colours*

There are basically four different types of food colours used in this book: liquid food colours, paste food colours, blossom tints or dusting colours and edible lustre or pearl spray. Each has its appropriate uses and advantages, and produces a slightly different effect.

LIQUID FOOD COLOURS

These usually come in squeeze bottles and are less concentrated. They are perfect for colouring liquid fondant or runny royal icing. Always add the colour first before adding more liquid to your fondant or royal icing as it can change the consistency.

PASTE FOOD COLOURS

Sold in jars, paste colour is perfect for colouring royal icing for piping and sugar paste or sugar florist paste. As it is very concentrated you will only need a small amount to achieve the required colour. Always mix the colour to a slightly lighter shade than you are aiming for as it usually darkens slightly once dry.

BLOSSOM TINTS/DUSTING COLOURS

These come in jars and are used for brushing sugar flower petals and other sugar decorations. They are applied in their dry versions using an artist's brush. They can also be mixed with a small amount of water to create a liquid paint.

EDIBLE LUSTRE/PEARL SPRAY

These are powders or sprays that impart a beautiful satiny shimmer. The powder can be brushed on to the sugar decorations or icing either dry or mixed with clear alcohol or piping gel to create a paint.

baking Cookies

The recipes for cookies and cakes that I have developed during the past couple of years produce results that not only taste delicious, but also have a very good texture, and – although light – are solid enough to provide an ideal base for decoration. It is important that you follow each recipe carefully, as baking requires time and patience. As important as it is to master the techniques, it is equally important to use only the best ingredients available, such as organic butter and eggs, real vanilla extract and high-quality preserves and liqueurs.

**MAKES ABOUT 25 MEDIUM-SIZE
OR 12 LARGE COOKIES**

sugar Cookies

Baking temperature: 180°C, gas 4;
baking time: 6–10 minutes,
    depending on size

INGREDIENTS
200g unsalted soft butter
200g caster sugar
1 egg, lightly beaten
400g plain flour, plus more for
    dusting

EQUIPMENT
electric mixer with paddle
    attachment
cling-film
pair of marzipan spacers
large rolling pin
cookie cutters in appropriate shapes

small palette knife
baking tray
greaseproof paper
wire cooling rack

OPTIONAL FLAVOURS
for vanilla cookies, add seeds from 1
    vanilla pod
for lemon cookies, add finely grated
    zest of 1 lemon
for orange cookies, add finely
    grated zest of 1 orange
for chocolate cookies, replace 50g
    of the plain flour with 50g cocoa
    powder

1 In the electric mixer with paddle attachment, cream the butter, sugar and chosen flavouring until well mixed and just becoming creamy in texture. Don't overwork, or the cookies will spread during baking.

2 Beat in the egg until well combined. Add the flour and mix on low speed until a dough forms (see 1). Gather it into a ball, wrap it in cling film and chill it for at least 1 hour.

3 Place the dough on a floured surface and knead it briefly. Using marzipan spacers, roll it out to an even thickness (see 2).

1

— 2

3

4 Use cookie cutters to cut out the desired shapes (see 3) and, using a palette knife, lay these on a baking tray lined with greaseproof paper. Chill again for about 30 minutes and preheat the oven to 180°C/gas 4.

5 Bake for 6–10 minutes. depending on size, until golden brown at the edges. Leave to cool on a wire rack. Wrapped in foil or cling film, they will keep well in a cool dry place for up to a month.

TIP: Always bake equally sized cookies together to make sure they cook in the same time. If you mix different sizes, the smaller ones are already cooked when the larger ones are still raw in the middle.

MAKES ABOUT 40 MEDIUM-SIZE
OR 20 LARGE COOKIES

gingerbread *Cookies*

Baking temperature: 200°C, gas 6; baking time: 8–12 minutes, depending on size

INGREDIENTS
250g cold salted butter, diced
1 teaspoon bicarbonate of soda
560g plain flour

FOR THE HOT MIX
5 tablespoons water

210g brown sugar
3 tablespoons treacle
3 tablespoons golden syrup
3 tablespoons ground ginger
3 tablespoons ground cinnamon
1 teaspoon ground cloves

EQUIPMENT
deep heavy saucepan
wooden spoon or plastic spatula
electric mixer with paddle attachment

sieve
cling film
pair of marzipan spacers
rolling pin
cookie cutters in appropriate shapes
small palette knife
baking tray
greaseproof paper
wire cooling rack

GINGERBREAD COOKIES (CONTINUED)

1 Place all the ingredients for the hot mix in a deep heavy saucepan and bring to the boil, stirring (see 1).

2 Once boiled, remove the pan from the heat and, using a wooden spoon or plastic spatula, carefully stir in the diced butter (see 2).

3 Once these are well combined, add the bicarbonate of soda and whisk the mix through briefly.

4 Pour into the bowl of the electric mixer and allow to cool until just slightly warm.

5 Once the mixture has cooled, sieve the flour over the top and start combining the two on a low speed, using the paddle attachment, until it forms a wet and sticky dough (see 3).

6 Wrap the dough in cling-film and chill for a couple of hours or overnight.

7 Place the chilled dough on a floured clean surface and knead it through briefly.

8 Place the kneaded dough between a pair of marzipan spacers and roll it out to an even thickness.

9 Use the cookie cutters to cut out the desired shapes and lay them on a baking tray lined with greaseproof paper.

10 Chill again for about 30 minutes. Preheat the oven to 200°C, gas 6.

11 Bake the cookies in the preheated oven for about 8-12 minutes, depending on the cookie size, until just firm to the touch.

12 Lift off the tray and allow to cool on a wire rack. Wrapped in foil or cling film, they will keep well in a cool dry place for up to a month.

TIPS

Cookie dough or uncooked cookies can be wrapped in cling-film and stored in the freezer for up to 3 months.

Cookies baked from frozen hold better in shape as they don't tend to spread as much as chilled ones.

Baked sugar cookies will keep for up to 1 month and gingerbread cookies up to 3 months, if kept in an airtight container or cookie jar.

baking Cakes

While traditional Victoria sponge and Rich dark chocolate cake are still the most popular choices for large cakes as well as cup cakes and fondant fancies, I have been finding there is increasing demand for more adventurous types of cake, such as the carrot cake for the slightly more health-conscious, and the marble cake, because it looks so stunning when sliced open. I have also recently widened my repertoire of fillings so that my cakes are just as exciting to bite into as they are to look at.

lining Cake Tins

1

EQUIPMENT
square or round cake tin of the
    required size
greaseproof paper
pencil
pair of scissors

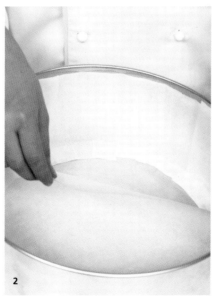

2

1 Place the cake tin on top of the greaseproof paper, draw a line around the base with a pencil and use that as a guide to cut out a piece to line the base.

2 Then cut out a strip that is about 5cm wider than the depth of your tin and long enough to line the inside edge. Fold 2.5cm of this strip over along its length and cut little snips along the folded edge up to the crease.

3 Place the long paper strip with the snipped edge at the bottom inside the tin to cover the sides (see 1).

4 Now place the paper base on top and make sure the snips and the base are forming a sharp corner and won't allow any dough to leak through the paper lining (see 2). For square tins, use the same technique as above, but fold the long strip that covers the sides at the four corners to fit neatly inside the tin (see 1).

MAKES ONE 20CM SPONGE CAKE ($^1/_2$ A TIER),
25 FONDANT FANCIES OR 20-24 CUP CAKES

victoria *Sponge*

Baking temperature: 180°C, gas 4;
baking time: 12-15 minutes for cup
cakes, 20-45 minutes for large
cakes, depending on size

INGREDIENTS
200g salted butter, softened
200g caster sugar
4 medium eggs
200g self-raising flour
100ml sugar syrup (see page 118),
   flavoured to your choice

EQUIPMENT
electric mixer with a paddle
   attachment
mixing bowl
20cm cake tin for large cake or
   fondant fancies, muffin trays
   and muffin cases for cup cakes
wooden skewer
greaseproof paper
large palette knife (for large cakes
   and fondant fancies)
small spoon or large plastic piping
   bag (for cup cakes)
wire cooling rack
pastry brush

For other sizes and quantities, please
refer to the guide on page 138.

OPTIONAL FLAVOURS
For vanilla sponge, add the seeds of
   1 vanilla pod
For lemon sponge, add the finely
   grated zest of 2 lemons
For orange sponge, add the finely
   grated zest of 2 oranges

1 Preheat the oven to 180°C, gas 4.

2 Place the butter, sugar and chosen
flavouring in an electric mixer and,
using the paddle, cream together
until pale and fluffy.

3 Beat the eggs lightly in another
bowl and slowly add to the mix,
while paddling on medium speed.
If the mixture starts curdling, add
a little bit of flour.

4 Once the eggs and the butter
mixture are combined, mix in the
flour at low speed.

5 Line the required baking tin as
explained on the previous page. For
cup cakes, place the paper cases
into the muffin trays.

6 Spread the dough evenly into the
tin using a palette knife (see 1 and 2).
TIP: As sponge always rises more in
the centre, spread it slightly higher

around the edge. For cup cakes, fill the paper cases about two-thirds full, using a small spoon or a plastic piping bag.

7 Bake for 12-15 minutes for cup cakes and 20-45 minutes for large cakes, depending on size. The sponge is cooked when it springs back to the touch and the sides are coming away from the tin. Alternatively, you can check it by inserting the tip of a clean thin knife into the centre; it should come out clean.

8 Once the sponge is baked, let it rest for about 15 minutes.

9 Prick the top of the sponge with a wooden skewer and, using a pastry brush, soak it with the syrup, while the sponge is still warm.

10 For cup cakes, wait about 10 minutes after baking before soaking the cup cakes with the sugar syrup. This way they will absorb the syrup immediately and not seem dry.

11 Once cool, remove the cake from the tin and cool on wire rack.

12 For large cakes, once cool, wrap the sponge in greaseproof paper and then foil, then store in a cool dry place overnight. I prefer to let sponges rest overnight as they tend

to crumble if cut, layered and iced on the same day of baking.

13 Sponges and cup cakes have a shelf-life of up to 7 days after icing, and are suitable for freezing. If wrapped well, they can be frozen for up to 1 month.

TIP: Bake cup cakes on the day they'll be iced, as they dry out faster.

**MAKES ONE 20CM CAKE
OR 20-24 CUP CAKES**

rich dark *Chocolate* cake

Baking temperature: 160°C, gas 3; baking time: about 15 minutes for cup cakes, 25–45 minutes for large cakes, depending on size

INGREDIENTS
75g dark couverture chocolate drops
100ml milk
225g brown sugar
75g salted butter, softened
2 medium eggs, slightly beaten
150g plain flour
1½ tablespoons cocoa powder
½ teaspoon baking powder
½ teaspoon bicarbonate of soda

EQUIPMENT
20cm cake tin for large cake or
    fondant fancies, muffin trays and
    cases for cup cakes
greaseproof paper
deep saucepan
electric mixer with a paddle
    attachment
sieve
mixing bowl
measuring jug
rubber spatula or wooden spoon

For other sizes and quantities, please refer to the guide on page 138. This cake is a little bit more moist than most other chocolate cake recipes, but it is also denser and slightly heavier at the same time, which makes it an excellent base for tiered cakes. It has a shelf-life of up to 10 days after icing.

1 Preheat the oven to 160°C, gas 3.

2 Line the required baking tin as described on page 113. For cup cakes place the muffin paper cases into the muffin trays.

3 Place the chocolate, milk and half the sugar in a deep span and bring to the boil, stirring occasionally.

4 Using an electric mixer with a paddle attachment, beat the butter and remaining sugar until pale and fluffy.

5 Slowly add the eggs.

6 Sift the flour, cocoa powder, baking powder and bicarbonate of soda and add to the mixture while mixing at a low speed.

7 While the chocolate mix is still hot, using a measuring jug, slowly pour it into the dough while mixing at low speed (see 1).

8 Once combined (see 2), pour the mix from the bowl directly into the lined tin (see 3). For cup cakes, first transfer the cake mix into a jug, as it is very liquid, and fill the cases about two-thirds full.

9 Bake for 15 minutes for cup cakes, 25–45 minutes for large cakes, depending on size. It is cooked when it springs back to the touch and the sides are coming away from the tin. Or, insert a clean kitchen knife into the centre; it should come out clean.

10 Once the cake is/cup cakes are baked, let it rest for about 15 minutes. Once cool, remove the cake(s) from the tin.

11 For storage, wrap in greaseproof paper and then in foil and store in a cool dry place overnight. I let sponges rest overnight as they tend to crumble if baked, cut, layered and iced on the same day. For cup cakes, I recommend baking on the same day they will be iced, as they tend to dry out faster. This cake is suitable for freezing. Wrapped well, it can be frozen for up to 3 months.

**MAKES ONE
20CM CAKE**

Carrot cake

Baking temperature: 180°C/gas 4
baking time: about 20 minutes

INGREDIENTS
90g butter
200g carrots, grated
50g chopped hazelnuts, toasted
180g soft light-brown sugar
2 large eggs
200g plain flour
1½ teaspoons baking powder
½ teaspoon baking soda
1 teaspoon ground cinnamon

EQUIPMENT
grater
sieve
bowls
small saucepan (optional)
electric mixer with paddle
    attachment
rubber spatula or wooden spoon
20cm cake tin
wire cooling rack
greaseproof paper
metal foil
kitchen knife

1

2

1 Melt the butter in a saucepan or in a suitable container in the microwave cooker and let it cool.

2 Grate the carrots, and put with the nuts and sugar in the bowl of an electric mixer and beat in the eggs at a medium speed, followed by the cool molten butter.

3 Sift the flour, baking powder and soda, and the cinnamon into the batter and mix at low speed until combined. Pour into the lined tin.

4 Bake in the preheated oven for about 20 minutes. The cake is cooked when it springs back to the touch and the sides are coming away from the tin. Alternatively, insert a clean knife into the centre and it should come out clean.

5 Once baked, let it rest for about 20 minutes before removing it from the tin and letting cool on a wire rack.

6 I let it rest overnight as they can crumble if baked, cut, layered and iced on the same day. Wrap in greaseproof paper, then in foil and store in a cool dry place. It has a shelf-life of 3-4 days after icing. It is suitable for freezing; wrapped well, it can be frozen for up to 3 months.

Marble cake

Baking temperature 180°C/gas 4; baking time: about 20-45 minutes

INGREDIENTS

FOR THE VANILLA MIX
100g salted butter, softened
100g caster sugar
2 medium eggs
100g self-raising flour

FOR THE CHOCOLATE MIX
100g salted butter, softened
100g caster sugar
2 medium eggs
70g self-raising flour
30g cocoa powder
pinch of baking powder

100ml vanilla sugar syrup (page 119)

EQUIPMENT
baking tin in required size and shape
greaseproof paper
electric mixer with paddle attachment
sieve
bowls
rubber spatula or wooden spoon
tablespoon
fork or truffle dipping fork
pastry brush
wire cooling rack
kitchen knife

1 Line a baking tin with greaseproof paper as described on page 113.

2 Prepare the vanilla mix as for the Victoria sponge, page 114, steps 1-4.

3 For the chocolate mix, repeat Victoria sponge, steps 1-3, then sift the flour, cocoa powder and baking powder together, add it the batter and mix it together at a low speed.

4 Spread the mix into the lined tin first using a palette knife, then spread the vanilla mix on top (see 1).

5 With a tablespoon, fold through bit by bit (see 2), then run a fork through for marbling effect (see 3).

6 Bake for 20-45 minutes. Test if done with a knife as in Carrot cake (previous page).

7 Continue as for steps 8–12 of Victoria sponge.

MAKES 100ML

sugar *Syrups*

Roughly the amount needed for a 20cm layered cake tier, a 30cm single tier square sponge to make 25 fondant fancies, or 20-24 cup cakes.

INGREDIENTS

FOR VANILLA SYRUP
5 tablespoons water
75g sugar
seeds from ½ vanilla pod or
    1 teaspoon Madagascan vanilla
    essence

FOR LEMON SYRUP
5 tablespoons freshly squeezed
    lemon juice
75g sugar
1 tablespoon Limoncello liqueur

FOR ORANGE SYRUP
5 tablespoons freshly squeezed
    orange juice
75g sugar
1 tablespoon Grand Marnier liqueur

EQUIPMENT
deep saucepan
spatula

1 Place the water or juice and sugar in a deep saucepan and bring to the boil. Remove from the heat and allow it to cool.

2 Once cool, stir in the flavourings.

3 Ideally, let the syrup infuse overnight as this will bring out the most of the flavours.

4 To store sugar syrup, keep it in an airtight bottle or container inside the fridge and it will last for up to 1 month.

Buttercream frosting

Roughly the amount you will need to layer a 20cm cake tier

INGREDIENTS
250g unsalted butter, softened
250g icing sugar, sifted
pinch of salt

OPTIONAL FLAVOURS
For vanilla buttercream (see 4), add the seeds of 1 vanilla pod
For lemon (see 3), add the finely grated zest of 2 lemons
For orange (see 1), add the finely grated zest of 2 oranges
For strawberry (see 2), add 2 tablespoons good strawberry jam and a tiny drop of pink food colour
For chocolate (see 5), replace half the buttercream with chocolate ganache (opposite)

For mocha buttercream, add a double shot of cool espresso to the chocolate buttercream

EQUIPMENT
electric mixer with a paddle attachment

For other sizes and quantities please refer to the guide on page 138.

Following a traditional English recipe, I use equal quantities of butter and icing sugar to make my buttercream. The method is very simple and, as it is an egg-free recipe, it has a longer shelf-life than most other buttercreams.

1 Place the butter, icing sugar, salt and flavouring in the bowl of an electric mixer and, using the paddle attachment, bring the mixture together on low speed. Turn the speed up and beat until light and fluffy.

2 If not using it immediately, store in a sealed container in the fridge and bring it back to room temperature before use. It has a shelf-life of up to 2 weeks if refrigerated.

belgian Chocolate Ganache

1

2

3

Roughly the amount you will need to layer a 20cm cake tier

INGREDIENTS
500g dark couverture chocolate
drops (minimum 53% cocoa
content)
500ml single cream

EQUIPMENT
heatproof mixing bowl
saucepan
whisk

For other sizes and quantities please refer to the guide on page 138.

1 Place the chocolate drops in a bowl.

2 Place the cream in a saucepan, stir well and heat it up to a bare simmer.

3 Pour the hot cream over the chocolate (see 1) and whisk them together until smooth (see 2 and 3). Don't over-whisk the ganache, as it can split quite easily.

4 Cool slightly until just setting before use. It can be stored in a sealed container in the fridge for up to a month.

layering and icing *Cakes*

Tiered cakes, as well as miniature cakes, provide the option of mixing different flavours of cakes. If you would like to make a tiered cake with different flavours, you have to bear in mind that the bottom tier has to carry the weight of the other tiers and therefore a stronger cake base should be used for the bottom tiers and lighter cakes for the top. For example, if you use my recipes, I recommend using chocolate cake for the lower tiers and the lighter Victoria sponge-based cakes for the upper tiers. You will find a full portion guide and charts indicating amounts of basic cake mixtures, fillings and covering required for various types and sizes of cakes on page 138. A template for the positioning of dowels to support cake tiers is also given at the back of the book.

**MAKES 8-10 DESSERT-SIZED
MINIATURE CAKES**

Miniature cakes

I usually bake and layer miniature cakes 3 days in advance, ice them the next day and add the decoration the day before. The illustrations opposite show a marble cake with buttercream filling, but they can be made with any cake or filling.

INGREDIENTS
30cm square sponge cake (page 114)

FOR THE FILLING:
about 4 heaped tablespoons jam, marmalade, lemon curd, buttercream (page 120) or ganache (page 121)
small amount of icing sugar for dusting
about 600g buttercream or ganache (page 121), flavoured to your choice
1.5kg marzipan
1.5kg sugar paste
100ml sugar syrup (page 119), flavoured to your choice
small amount of clear alcohol (I use vodka as it has a neutral taste) or water

EQUIPMENT
cake leveller or large serrated knife
small palette knife
thin cake cards to match the number, size and shape of your chosen miniature cakes
pastry brush
cling-film
large rolling pin
7.5cm round high pastry cutter and/or 5 x 7.5cm oval cutter
icing sugar sieve
pair of marzipan spacers
small kitchen knife

1 Using a cake leveller or large serrated knife, trim the top crust off your sponge (see 1, previous page).

2 Using the cutters, cut 16 rounds or 20 ovals from the sheet of sponge (see 2).

3 Place half of them on the cake cards with a dab of buttercream or ganache and soak the tops with sugar syrup (see 3).

4 Using a small palette knife, spread them with a layer of the filling (see 4) and place the other sponges on top of them.

5 Again, soak the tops of the sponges with sugar syrup.

6 Cover each mini cake all around with buttercream or ganache (see 5) and chill until set and feeling nice

7 Once set, on a smooth surface lightly dusted with icing sugar, roll out the marzipan using spacers to get an even thickness. Cut the marzipan into squares that are large enough to cover the cakes.

8 Cover one cake at a time with the marzipan and gently push it down the sides (see 6). Avoid tearing the edges. Trim off excess using a kitchen knife.

9 Polish the sides and tops of each cake with the cake smoothers (see 7).

10 Let the marzipan set for a few hours or preferably overnight.

11 Once the marzipan is set, brush each cake with a thin layer of clear alcohol.

12 Repeat steps 7 to 9 (see pics 8 and 9 on the previous page), using the sugar paste instead of marzipan. Let dry completely, preferably overnight.

MY FAVOURITE CAKE AND FILLING COMBINATIONS

- Vanilla sponge, soaked with vanilla syrup, layered with raspberry preserve and vanilla buttercream
- Lemon sponge, soaked with lemon and Limoncello syrup, layered with lemon curd and lemon buttercream
- Orange sponge, soaked with orange and Grand Marnier syrup, layered with luxury orange marmalade and orange buttercream
- Rich dark chocolate cake layered with Belgian chocolate ganache
- Vanilla sponge, soaked with morello cherry jam
- Rich dark chocolate cake layered with vanilla buttercream and mocha buttercream
- Vanilla sponge layered with vanilla, strawberry and chocolate buttercream
- Carrot cake layered with lemon buttercream
- Marble cake soaked with vanilla syrup and layered with vanilla buttercream

MAKES ONE 20CM ROUND CAKE TIER

Large cakes

1

2

3

4

For a 20cm round cake tier you will need two 20cm round sponges (see the quantities guide on page 138).

INGREDIENTS

about 600g buttercream or ganache, jam, marmalade or lemon curd (for Victoria sponge only)

about 200ml sugar syrup (for Victoria sponge and Marble cake only)

icing sugar for dusting

about 850g marzipan

small amount of clear alcohol (I use vodka as it has a neutral taste)

about 850g sugar paste

EQUIPMENT

cake leveller or large serrated knife

small kitchen knife

20cm round cake board

large palette knife

pastry brush

metal side scraper

turntable

icing sugar sieve

large rolling pin

pair of marzipan spacers

pair of cake smoothers

scriber

1 Using the leveller or serrated knife, trim the top and bottom crusts off both sponges.

2 Slice each sponge in half so you have 4 layers of the same depth (about 2cm each).

3 Place the cake board on the turntable and spread with a thin layer of buttercream or ganache. Put the first sponge layer on top and soak with sugar syrup if required (see 1).

4 Spread the sponge with buttercream or ganache, put the second layer on top (see 2). Soak with syrup.

5 Keep on layering the remaining pieces of sponge in this way with preserves or buttercream or ganache until all 4 layers are assembled. Press the layers down gently but firmly to ensure that the cake is level (see 3).

6 Using a large palette knife, coat the outside of the cake with buttercream or ganache (see 4). Start spreading from the top centre

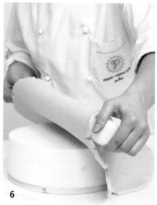

5   6   7   8

and towards the edge as you are rotating the turntable.

7 Push the buttercream down the sides and spread it evenly all around the sides.

8 Use a metal side scraper to clean up the sides (see 5) and do the same on the top with a palette knife.

9 Chill for at least 2 hours or overnight until the cake has set and feels firm.

10 Once set, dust a working surface with icing sugar, place the marzipan on top and, using the marzipan spacers, roll out to an even round large enough to cover the top and sides.

11 Lift the marzipan with the rolling pin, lay it over the cake (see 6) and gently push it down the sides. Trim off any excess marzipan using the kitchen knife.

12 Polish the marzipan with the cake smoothers (see 7) and use the palms of your hands to smooth the edges. Let the marzipan set, preferably overnight.

13 Once set, brush the marzipan with a thin coat of clear alcohol to stick on the sugar paste icing. The alcohol not only destroys any bacteria that may have built up while storing the cake, but it also evaporates within minutes after its application and therefore creates a strong and hygienic glue between the marzipan and the sugar paste. Should you prefer not to use alcohol, you can use boiled cold water instead.

14 Repeat steps 10 to 12 using sugar paste instead of marzipan (see 8).

TIPS: For tiered cakes, start the preparation about 5 to 6 days before the event. For example, if the wedding is on a Saturday, bake the sponges on the Monday before and layer them on the Tuesday. Cover the cakes with marzipan on Wednesday and leave overnight, so that the marzipan has time to dry. On Thursday, cover the cakes with sugar paste and let them set again overnight. This gives you the whole

of Friday to apply your decorations, which you can prepare a couple of weeks in advance.

For single tiered cakes, start about 3 to 4 days before the event, as the cake can be covered with marzipan and sugar paste on the same day. To make one cake tier you need two sponges of the same size.

For a well-proportioned tiered cake, each tier should ideally be about 8.5cm high, including the cake board, before applying the marzipan and icing. Make sure that all tiers have the exact same height unless a mixture of different heights is intended.

covering
Cake Boards

Ice your cake board at least 1 or 2 days ahead, to ensure that the icing is well set before placing the cake on top.

INGREDIENTS
icing sugar for dusting
small amount of clear alcohol
sugar paste (see the quantity guide on page 138)

EQUIPMENT
thick cake board of the required size
pastry brush
rolling pin
cake smoother

small kitchen knife
15mm wide satin ribbon to cover the sides
double-sided sticky tape

1 Dust the cake board thinly with icing sugar and brush it with a little alcohol (to make a glue for the sugar paste).

2 Roll the sugar paste out to about 3mm thick and large enough to cover the cake board.

3 Use the rolling pin, lift the paste and lay it over the board (see 1).

4 Let the cake smoother glide carefully over the surface of the paste and push out any air bubbles.

5 Lift the board with one hand and push the paste down the side with the smoother in the other hand (see 2).

6 Trim the excess paste off with a sharp kitchen knife (see 3) and let the sugar paste dry for 1 to 2 days.

7 Once the paste is dry, wind the ribbon around the edge of the board and fix the ends with double-sided sticky tape.

assembling *Tiered Cakes*

INGREDIENTS

cake tiers of different sizes, covered
with marzipan and sugar paste
iced cake board about 7.5-10cm
larger than the bottom tier
royal icing (see page 132)
small amount of sugar paste the
same colour as the icing
small amount of water

EQUIPMENT

plastic dowels (4 for each tier except
the top one)
palette knife
serrated kitchen knife
pair of strong scissors
food colour pen
dowel template (page 144)
paper piping bag (page 134)
small bowl
damp cloth
spirit level
pair of tweezers

1 Using a palette knife, spread the
centre of the iced board with a thin
layer of royal icing that doesn't
exceed the size of the bottom tier.

2 Carefully lift your bottom tier with
the palette knife and centre it on
top of the cake board (see 1).

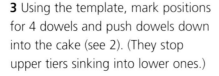

3 Using the template, mark positions
for 4 dowels and push dowels down
into the cake (see 2). (They stop
upper tiers sinking into lower ones.)

4 With a food colour pen, mark
each dowel about 1mm above the
point at which it comes out of the
cake.

5 Carefully remove the dowels, line them up next to one another and cut to the same length, using the average mark as a guide line. Stick them back in the cake. To see if they all have the same height, place a cake board on top of them and check that it sits straight, ideally using a small spirit level. Should you have to readjust the length of a dowel, carefully pull it out of the cake with tweezers and trim it with scissors then replace.

6 Once happy with the dowels, spread a little icing in the middle of the cake, carefully lift the second tier with your palette knife and centre it on top of the bottom tier.

7 Repeat steps 3 to 6 for the second and third tiers if required.

8 Once all your tiers are assembled, mix the sugar paste with water to a thick but smooth paste. Put in a paper piping bag and squeeze into the gaps between tiers to fill them.

9 Dampen your finger with a damp cloth and run it along the filled gaps to wipe off excess paste.

TIP: Depending on transportation and distance to the event, it may be safer to assemble a tiered cake on site.

MAKES 25 FONDANT FANCIES

dipping
Fondant Fancies

Liquid fondant is widely used as a filling for chocolate truffles, etc., or as a glaze for pastries. It has a very long shelf-life and tastes deliciously smooth when flavoured with fruit juices, essences or liqueurs. As it is white, it provides an ideal base for mixing brilliant colours. Made by boiling together sugar, glucose syrup and water, it requires experience and skill to achieve the right consistency. To keep it simple, I use ready-made fondant.

INGREDIENTS
20cm square Victoria sponge, well soaked with syrup (pages 114-5), trimmed and layered with the filling of your choice (pages 120-1)

1 heaped tablespoon sieved apricot jam
icing sugar for dusting
about 150g marzipan
about 1kg ready-made liquid fondant
small amount of liquid glucose
selection of liquid food colours (optional)

EQUIPMENT
tray
cling-film
pastry brush
large rolling pin
small knife
microwave cooker
small microwaveable bowls
truffle fork
wire cooling rack
25 silver muffin cases (optional)

1 Wrap your layered sponge cake well in cling-film and chill it for at least an hour or so, to give it time to firm up.

2 Once it is cool and firm, warm the apricot jam, unwrap the sponge and spread a thin layer of jam over the top, using the pastry brush.

3 On a work surface lightly dusted with icing sugar, knead the marzipan until smooth and pliable. Shape it into a ball and roll it out to a square large enough to cover the top of the sponge and about 3mm thick.

4 Carefully lift it and lay it over the top of the cake. Trim the excess, if necessary.

5 Slice the marzipan-topped sponge into 4cm squares and spread the tops with a thin layer of jam (see 1 on the previous page).

6 Put the fondant in a large microwaveable bowl and gently heat it in the microwave cooker at medium heat for about 1 minute. Stir in the glucose and heat it again

for about 20 seconds at a time, until it is warm and runny. (Alternatively, heat it in a saucepan over very low heat, stirring. Do not allow the fondant to boil, or it will lose its shine when cool again.) If necessary, you can add a little sugar syrup to it to make it more liquid (you are looking for a thick pouring consistency).

7 If you would like to mix the fondant with different colours, divide it between some bowls and add a few drops of food colour at a time until you achieve the desired shades.

8 Dip one cake at a time upside down into the fondant (see 2), until about three-quarters of the sides are covered. To lift out, hold with two fingers at the bottom and a truffle fork at the top (see 3), ensuring you don't push the fork into the

marzipan as it may tear it off. Quickly shake off excess icing and place the cake on the cooling rack (see 4). Leave it for the icing to set.

9 Carefully remove the fancies from the rack by cutting them loose at the bottom using a small kitchen knife and place in the cases. This is best done with slightly wet fingers, to prevent the icing sticking to them. Gently push the sides of the paper case against the sides of the cake and, as they stick, they take on the square shape. Place the cakes closely next to each other until ready for decoration. Again, this will help the cases stay square if required.

10 Iced fondant fancies keep for about 7 days in a cake box or wrapped in foil. Don't store them in the fridge or the icing will melt.

dipping
Cup Cakes

INGREDIENTS

2–3 heaped tablespoons sieved
   apricot jam
20–24 well-soaked cup cakes (page
   114)
About 1kg ready-made liquid fondant
small amount of plain sugar syrup
1 heaped teaspoon liquid glucose
selection of food colours

EQUIPMENT

pastry brush
microwave cooker
small microwaveable bowls
small palette knife

1 Warm the jam and brush a thin layer over each cup cake to seal it (see 1).

2 Put the fondant in a large microwaveable bowl and gently heat in the microwave cooker at medium for 1 minute. Stir in the glucose and heat again for 20 seconds at a time, until warm and runny. (Or, heat in a pan over very low heat, stirring. Do not allow the fondant to boil, or it will lose its shine.) If necessary, add a little sugar syrup to make it more liquid (you are looking for a thick pouring consistency).

3 If you would like to mix the fondant with different colours, divide it between some bowls and add a few drops of colour at a time until you get the desired shades.

4 Dip all the cup cakes of one colour first into the fondant (see 2), shake off excess and let set before moving on to the next colour. By the time you have dipped the last cakes, the icing of the first will have set and you can begin with the second coat of icing, as before. Dipping each cake twice will ensure a beautifully smooth and shiny surface.

5 Leftover fondant can be stored in a bowl wrapped with cling-film. Before using again, pour hot water over the top to soften the hardened top and let soak for 15 minutes, pour off the water and heat as usual.

TIPS: Start by mixing lighter fondant shades first and then add more fondant and colour as required. An economic trick is to mix different coloured icings to achieve a new colour. Say, to make yellow, blue and green icing, start with yellow in one bowl and blue in another. Then mix these together to make green icing.

royal icing and *Piping*

Piping with royal icing is probably the most essential skill needed for most of my designs, particularly for decorating cookies. Made from icing sugar and either fresh egg white or dried powdered egg white, it also makes an excellent glue for fixing sugar flowers and other decorations on to cakes. Making royal icing is a very simple procedure; should you find it daunting, however, you can buy ready-made versions at specialist cake decorating suppliers.

MAKES ABOUT 1KG

Royal icing

STIFF-PEAK CONSISTENCY

For sticking together cake tiers or sticking decorations on to icing

SOFT-PEAK CONSISTENCY

For piping lines, dots and borders

RUNNY CONSISTENCY

For filling in the centre of spaces

INGREDIENTS

about 25g merriwhite (dried egg
    white powder) or whites of 4
    medium eggs
1 kg icing sugar, sifted
squeeze of lemon juice

EQUIPMENT

sieve
electric mixer with paddle
    attachment
wooden spoon or rubber spatula
sealable plastic container
J-cloth

1 If using the merriwhite, mix with water and use as per the packet instructions. Ideally, let this rest overnight in the fridge before use.

2 Place the sugar in the bowl of an electric mixer, add three-quarters of the merriwhite mix or the lightly beaten egg whites and the lemon juice. Start mixing on low speed.

3 Once well combined, check the consistency. If the sides of the bowl still look dry and crumbly, add some more merriwhite or egg white until the icing looks almost smooth but not wet.

4 Keep mixing on low speed for about 4-5 minutes, until it has reached stiff-peak consistency.

5 Spoon into a sealable plastic container, cover with a clean damp J-cloth and the lid. Store at room temperature for up to 7 days; if using fresh egg, store in the refrigerator. The egg white can separate from the sugar after a couple of days, which will turn the icing into a dry, dense mixture. In such a case, remix at low speed until smooth and at stiff-peak consistency again. Make sure that no dried icing bits sticking to the sides of your storage container get into the mixing bowl.

ROYAL ICING CONSISTENCIES

Throughout the book, I refer to the three useful consistencies of royal icing (as opposite), which are important in achieving the right results. Simply thin down your basic royal icing recipe with water, a little bit at a time, using a palette knife, until you have reached the right consistency. Always make sure you keep your icing covered with cling-film or a damp cloth when not using it, to stop it from drying out.

making a *Paper Piping Bag*

1

2

3

4

5

1 Take a rectangular piece of grease-proof paper, about 30x45cm, and cut it from one corner to the opposite one with scissors. Try sliding the scissors through the paper rather than cutting as this gives a cleaner cut.

2 Hold one of the resulting paper triangles with your hand at the middle of the longest side and with your other hand on the point on the opposite side. The longer side of the triangle should be on your left.

3 Curl the shorter corner on your right over to the corner that is pointing towards you, so that it forms a cone (see 1).

4 With your left hand, wrap the longer corner on the left around the tip of the cone twice and then join it together with the other 2 corners at the back of the cone (see 2 and 3).

5 If the bag still has an open tip at the front, you can close it by wiggling the inner and outer layers of paper back and forth, until the cone forms a sharp point (see 4).

6 Fold the corners at the open end into the inside of the bag twice to prevent it unravelling (see 5).

7 Only ever half-fill the bag or icing will ooze out when you squeeze. Close by folding the side with the seam over to the plain side twice.

TIP: For extra strength I use 'waxed' greaseproof paper, also called 'silicon paper', which I buy from a specialist baking supplier.

Piping techniques

The piping techniques demonstrated below are very useful to practise your general piping skills. Instead of piping directly on to a cake, simply take a piece of greaseproof paper and pipe on to that instead. You can also place templates underneath it and trace them through the paper with your piping bag. If you have never piped with royal icing before, this task is a great way to train your skills, after all practice makes perfect.

First snip a small tip off your piping bag already filled with icing. Hold the bag between the thumb and the fingers of your preferred hand and use the index finger of your other hand to guide the nozzle.

PIPING LINES:

1 Touch the starting point with the tip of the bag and slowly squeeze out the icing. As you are squeezing, lift the bag slightly and pull the line straight towards you or, for example, along the sides of a cookie.

2 Once you are approaching the finishing point, gradually bring the bag down, stop squeezing and drop the line by touching the finishing point with the tip of the bag.

PIPING DOTS:

1 Hold the tip of your piping bag 1mm above the surface and squeeze out the icing to produce a dot on the surface.

2 Gradually lift the tip as the dot gets larger.

3 Once the dot has reached its desired size, stop squeezing and lift off the tip.

4 Should the dot form a little peak at the top, flatten it carefully with a damp soft artist's brush.

PIPING LOOPS AND SWAGS:

1 Start as you would for piping lines.

2 Holding your bag at an angle of 45° to the surface, touch the starting point with the tip and slowly squeeze out the icing. As you squeeze, lift the bag up by about an inch and pull it from one side to the other in circular movements, overlapping the lines in even intervals to create evenly spaced loops and swags.

TIP: If you find it difficult to space

the loops and swags out evenly, mark the points where the loops will meet and use them as guides.

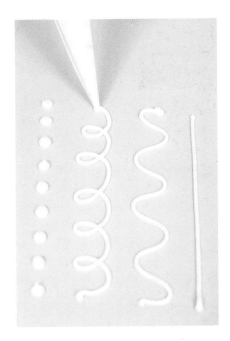

Glossary

Most items are available from specialist suppliers (opposite), although more everyday ones can be found in supermarkets and cookware shops.

INGREDIENTS

FONDANT Made from sugar, water and cream of tartar, fondant is widely used as a glaze in confectionery as well as in pâtisserie and cake decorating. Ready-made fondant is available in a block or as a powder to be mixed with water.

GLUCOSE, LIQUID A thick version of corn syrup used to make fondant icing in order to give it a beautiful shine.

GUM TRAGACANTH Made from the dried sap of the Astragalus plant, this is sold as a powdered hardening agent and is mixed with sugar paste to create a pliable modelling paste for making sugar flowers. It has the further effect of making the paste set on contact with air. It may also be mixed with a little water to make an edible glue.

LUSTRE (OR LUSTER), EDIBLE This non-toxic pearl dust comes in different shades. It can either be mixed to a thick paste with a drop of alcohol or applied directly with an artist's brush.

MARZIPAN Made from ground almonds and icing sugar, marzipan is used for covering large cakes before icing, as it seals in moisture as well as helping to stabilize shape. It is also ideal for making flowers, as it is very easy to mould and the individual petals stick to each other naturally.

MERRIWHITE This is dried egg white powder used instead of fresh egg whites in making royal icing for food safety reasons, as the dried egg white is pasteurized.

SUGAR FLORIST PASTE OR GUM PASTE A fine and pliable paste made from icing sugar, gelatine and gum tragacanth, which dries hard, with a porcelain-like texture. It is used to make finely crafted sugar flowers.

SUGAR PASTE A very smooth and pliable icing made from gelatin, icing sugar and water, which dries hard but is still easy to cut. Sugar paste is used for covering cakes and for making flowers and modelling cake decorations.

EQUIPMENT

BONE TOOL A long plastic stick with rounded ends, looking like a bone, this is used to shape sugar paste petals.

CAKE SMOOTHERS These are flat rectangular pieces of smooth plastic, with a handle, used to smooth the marzipan and sugar paste on a cake.

DESIGN WHEELER A plastic sugar craft tool with 3 interchangeable heads for creating patterns and designs, such as stitching, on sugar paste cakes.

DRESDEN TOOL A TOOL FOR FLUTING PETALS. ITS POINTED TIP IS USED TO EMPHASIZE FLOWER CENTRES, THE OTHER TO MAKE VEIN MARKINGS.

FLOWER CUTTERS Made of metal or plastic, flower cutters are used to cut petals and leaves out of flower paste.

In this book I have used cutters to make violets, hydrangeas and amenones.

FLOWER FOAM PAD This is used as a yielding surface for thinning the edges of flower paste with a bone tool (above).

FLOWER STAMEN Similar to the stamen used for silk flowers, these contain small wires and are used for sugar flower centres, although they are NOT edible.

LINEN-LOOK ROLLING PIN A plastic rolling pin with a textured surface that embosses a linen effect into icing.

MARZIPAN SPACERS Long sticks used to roll out dough, sugar paste or marzipan to an even thickness.

PETAL/LEAF VEINING MAT Rubber mat for shaping and marking leaves and petals.

PROFILE FOAM SHEET A sheet of textured packaging foam with wells (similar to a egg box); useful to support the shape of sugar flowers and leaves when drying.

SCRIBER NEEDLE A fine metal pin used to mark or scratch patterns into icing.

SIDE SCRAPER Flat piece of metal (ideally stainless steel) with a straight side used for scraping excess cream off the side of a cake when filling. It helps give perfectly straight sides.

SIDE SCRIBING/MARKING GAUGE A height-adjustable tool to scribe markings into icing in straight lines.

STAY FRESH MULTI MAT Thick acetate mat used to cover rolled-out sugar (flower) paste to prevent drying out.

Suppliers

FOR CAKE DECORATING TOOLS, FOOD COLOURS AND EQUIPMENT:

UK

Jane Asher Party Cakes
24 Cale Street
London SW3 3QU
www.jane-asher.co.uk

Almond Art
Unit 15/16
Faraday Close
Gorse Lane Industrial Estate
Clacton-on-Sea, Essex
CO15 4TR
tel 01255 223322
www.almondart.com

Squires Shop and School
Squires House
3 Waverley Lane
Farnham, Surrey
GU9 8BB
www.squires-group.co.uk

FOR FLOWER CUTTERS, VEINERS AND CAMEO MOULDS:

Design A Cake
30–31 Phoenix Road
Crowther Industrial Estate
Washington
Tyne & Wear
NE38 0AD
www.design-a-cake.co.uk

ASIA

International Centre of Cake Artistry Sdn. Bhd.
1-1 to 1-3A, Jalan PJU 5/15
Dataran Sunway
Kota Damansara
47810 Petaling Jaya,
Selangor, Malaysia
tel 603 6140 8835
www.2decoratecakes.com

AUSTRALIA & NEW ZEALAND

Cake Deco
Shop 7, Port Phillip Arcade
232 Flinders Street, Melbourne,
Victoria
Australia
www.cakedeco.com.au

Milly's
273 Ponsonby Road
Auckland,
New Zealand
tel 09 376 1550
www.millyskitchen.co.nz

GERMANY

Tortissimo Backzubehör
Carl-Benz-Str. 6
35305 Grünberg
Deutschland
www.tortissimo.de

THE NETHERLANDS

De Leukste Taarten Shop
Meeuwstraat 10
1546 LR Jisp, Holland
www.deleukstetaartenshop.nl

USA & CANADA

Global Sugar Art
28 Plattsburgh Plaza
Plattsburgh, NY 12901
tel 518 561 3039
www.globalsugarart.com

Creative Cutters
561 Edward Avenue, Unit 2
Richmond Hill, Ontario
Canada L4C 9W6
www.creativecutters.com

PEGGY PORSCHEN®
cakes

For more information on cake decorating classes and specialist equipment, or to place orders for Peggy Porschen's cookies and cakes, please visit her website peggyporschen.com

Quantity guides

CAKE MIX QUANTITY AND PORTION GUIDE

This chart will give an overview of what size cake you need for your number of guests and the approximate quantity of cake mix needed for the different sizes of cake tins.

The basic cake recipes in this book are based on a 20cm cake tin or 20–24 cup cakes or 25 fondant fancies. Please bear in mind that for each cake tier you will need 2 sponges, i.e. double the amount of cake mix, baked in 2 tins of the same size. The figure shown in the second column below indicates by how much the basic recipe needs to be multiplied.

CAKE TIN SIZE (ROUND OR SQUARE)	MULTIPLY BASIC RECIPE BY	CAKE PORTIONS 2.5x2.5CM (1x1 INCH) ROUND/SQUARE	MINI CAKES	CUP CAKES	FONDANT FANCIES
10cm (4 inch)	¼	10 / 16			
12.5cm (5 inch)	⅓	12 / 20			
15cm (6 inch)	½	20 / 35			
17.5cm (7 inch)	¾	25 / 45			
20cm (8 inch)	1	40 / 60	9	20-24	25
22.5cm (9 inch)	1⅓	50 / 80			
25cm (10 inch)	2	60 / 100	16	40-48	36
27.5cm (11 inch)	2½	80 / 120			
30cm (12 inch)	3¼	90 / 140	25		
35cm (14 inch)	4¼	130 / 185			

QUANTITY GUIDE FOR MARZIPAN AND SUGAR PASTE, AND BUTTERCREAM OR CHOCOLATE GANACHE FILLING

The figures below give you the approximate amounts required for cakes of different sizes, round or square, with a height of 8.5cm (3½ inches).

CAKE / BOARD SIZE	MARZIPAN / SUGAR PASTE	SUGAR PASTE FOR CAKE BOARD	BUTTERCREAM / GANACHE
10cm (4 inch)	400g		150g (also 25 fondant fancies)
12.5cm (5 inch)	500g		225g
15cm (6 inch)	600g	300g	300g
17.5cm (7 inch)	750g	400g	450g (also 20–24 cup cakes)
20cm (8 inch)	850g	600g	600g
22.5cm (9 inch)	1kg	700g	750g
25cm (10 inch)	1.25kg	800g	900g
27.5cm (11 inch)	1.5kg	850g	1.2kg
30cm (12 inch)	1.75kg	900g	1.5kg
32.5cm (13 inch)	2kg	950g	1.75kg
35cm (14 inch)	2.5kg	1kg	2kg

Index

Acknowledgements

Developing the concept for *Cake Chic* has been an absolute joy and I am incredibly proud of the result. The idea was to create a range of fabulously stylish cake designs and recipes that us girls would love to make not only for special occasions, but also to make any occasion a little bit special. The result is a truly gorgeous collection of couture cookies and cakes, and I hope that you will feel inspired by them – perhaps even discover a new talent – and have lots of fun when baking and creating these recipes.

Of course, like all books, it was a joint effort. I would like to thank the great team at Quadrille Publishing – Jane O'Shea, Helen Lewis and Katherine Case, headed by Alison Cathie! Thank you so much for all you support, input and creative guidance, and most importantly for sharing my vision for this wonderful new title. I hope you are all as delighted with the result as I am.

Another big thank-you goes to the rest of my hugely talented team, my lovely and infinitely patient editor Lewis Esson, the incredible photographer Georgia Glynn Smith, and the stylish stylist Vicky Sullivan – for all the love, dedication and inspiration you have brought to this project and for helping me to create this beautiful book.

To my new husband Bryn and my wonderful family – you give me the most incredible strength, love and support that I couldn't do without, and I owe everything to you!

The publishers would also like to thank the following for their invaluable assistance: Liberty Art Fabrics, London www.liberty.co.uk <www.liberty.co.uk%20> for permission to reproduce the fabric featured on the endpapers and on pages 43 and 45; Cole & Son www.cole-and-son.com <http://www.cole-and-son.com> for the Catwalk wallpaper featured on page 77; Farrow & Ball www.Farrow-Ball.com <http://www.Farrow-Ball.com> for their Spencer wallpaper featured on page 82; Joanna Wood www.joannawood.co.uk <http://www.joannawood.co.uk> for the plates, coffee cup and saucer featured on page 10; www.NewVintage.co.uk <http://www.NewVintage.co.uk> for the vintage china featured on pages 15, 43 and 45, and 61 and 63; Rice www.rice.dk <http://www.rice.dk> for the plates featured on pages 74-5.

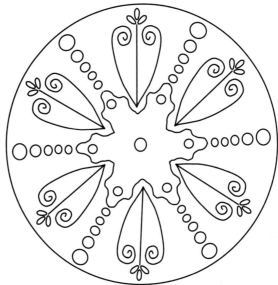

1 2 3
4 5 6 7
8 9 0

TEMPLATES FOR THE MINI MONOGRAM CAKES

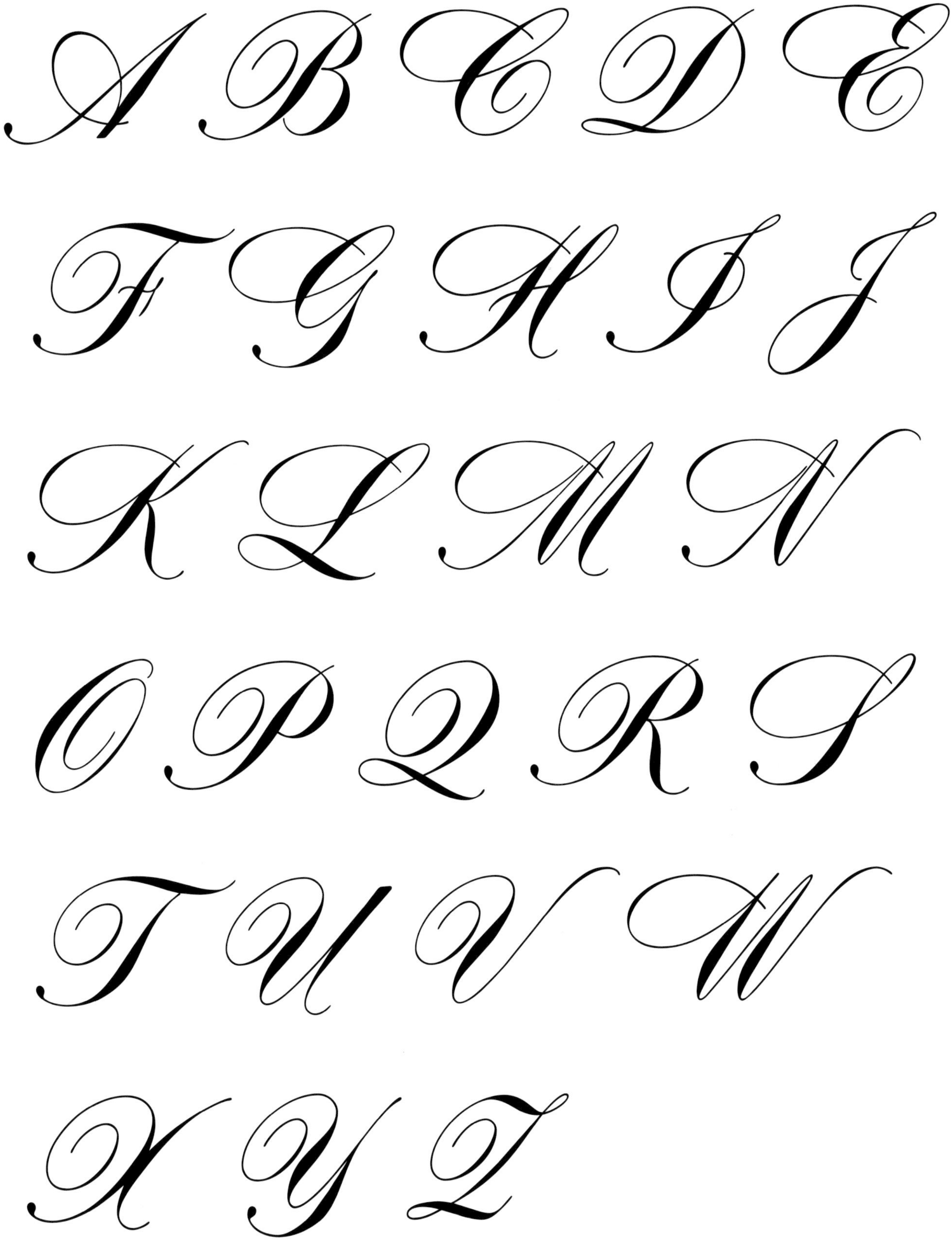

A B C D E

F G H I J

K L M N

O P Q R S

T U V W

X Y Z

143

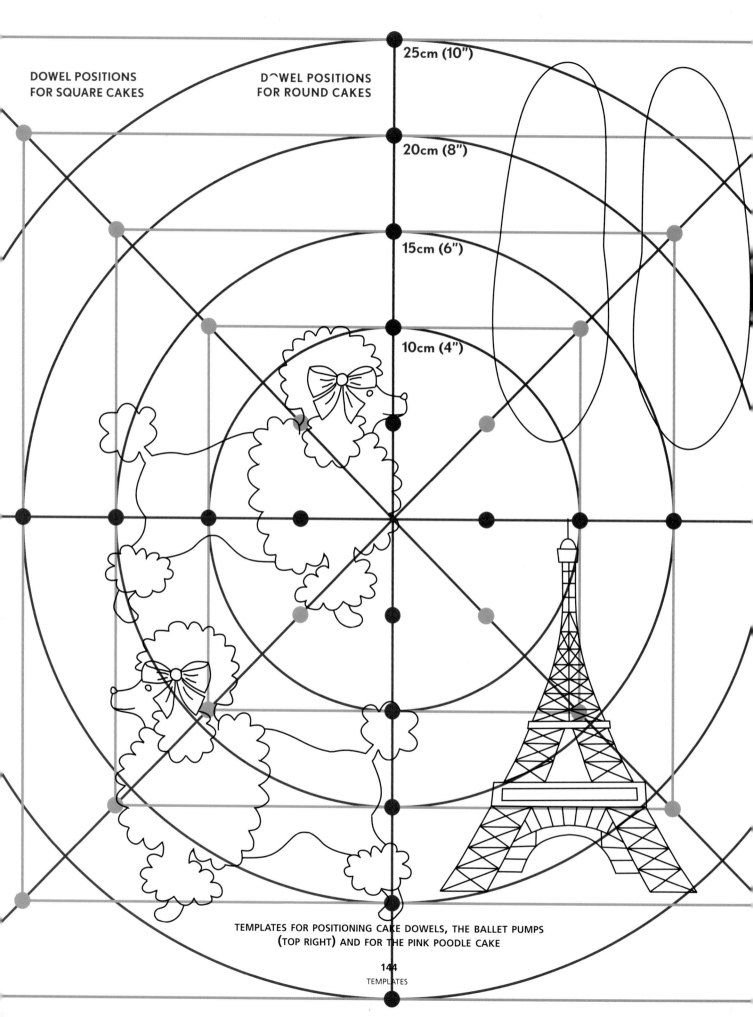

25cm (10")

20cm (8")

15cm (6")

10cm (4")

TEMPLATES FOR POSITIONING CAKE DOWELS, THE BALLET PUMPS
(TOP RIGHT) AND FOR THE PINK POODLE CAKE

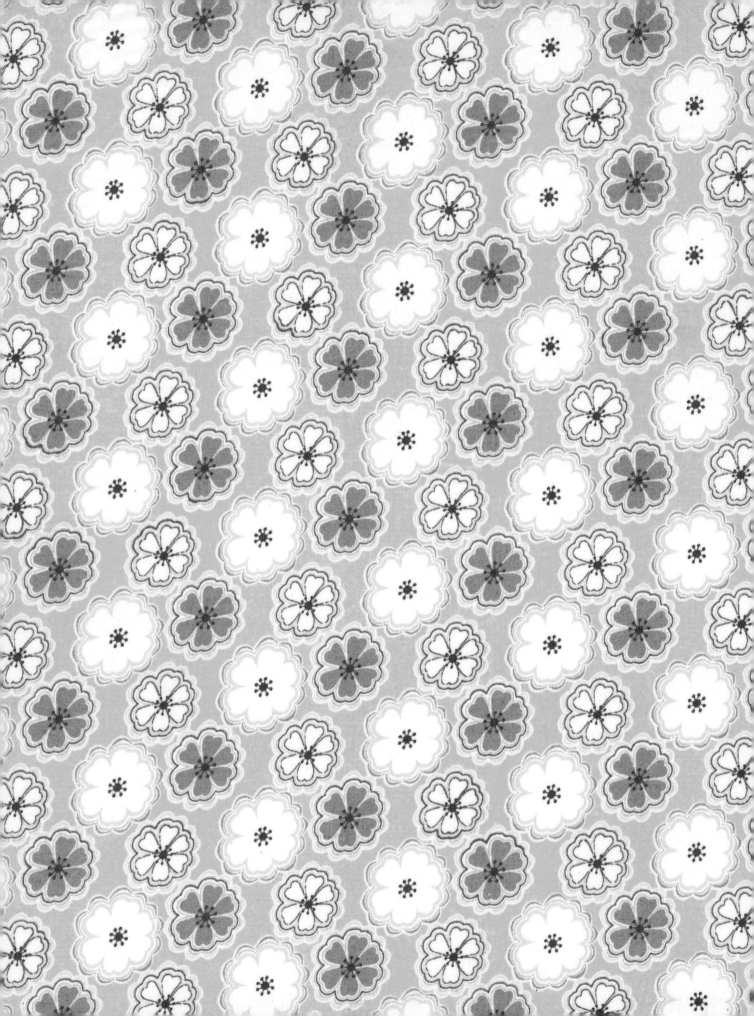